Heroes
from
American
History

A Content-Based Reader

Related titles by Anne Siebert:

Celebrating American Heroes: Plays for Students of English: The Playbook
Celebrating American Heroes: Teacher's Guide
Celebrating American Heroes: Cassette

Heroes
from
American History

A Content-Based Reader

Anne Siebert
Raymond C. Clark
illustrated by Marc Nadel

PRO LINGUA ⬤ ASSOCIATES

Pro Lingua Associates, Publishers

P.O.Box 1348
Brattleboro, Vermont 05302 USA
Office: 802 257 7779
Orders: 800 366 4775
Fax: 802 257 5117
E-mail: prolingu@sover.net
Web Store: www. ProLinguaAssociates.com
SAN: 216-0579

At Pro Lingua
our objective is to foster
an approach to learning and teaching
that we call **interplay**, *the* **inter**action *of language*
learners and teachers with their materials, with
the language and culture, and with
each other in active, creative
and productive **play**.

Copyright © 2002 Anne Siebert and Raymond C. Clark

ISBN 0-86647-143-X

This book was designed by Arthur A. Burrows. It was set in Electra with Apple Chancery display type, and it was printed and bound by Capital City Press in Montpelier, Vermont.

The illustrations are by Marc Nadel

Printed in the United States of America
First printing 2002. 3000 copies in print.

Contents

Foreword
to the teacher

This book with its readings and activities is intended to improve all of your students' English language skills. The "User's Guide," written for the students, explains each step of the work and the many skills involved. This reader also offers some important American history, focused on significant individuals and issues. The readings are intended to be provocative, to start students thinking critically, and to stimulate constructive discussion and writing. Although the language in this book is controlled, the history is full of challenges that are important to our lives today.

How can we make history exciting for students who are new to both our culture and language? To complement *Heroes from American History*, Anne Siebert has written a book of short plays titled *Celebrating American Heroes*. These plays tell the stories of thirteen of the heroes in this reader in a way that dramatically brings them to life and makes everyone involved in the plays care more about them and the history they were involved in. Although these two books can be used independently, they are designed to be used together.

Celebrating American Heroes is a play book with the script for each play. In each, the cast includes three or four major characters, a narrator, and a chorus, which comments on the action and interacts with the hero like the chorus in a Greek drama. All the students in class can be actively involved in reading or putting on their play.

A recording of a dramatic production of the plays is available for listening and pronunciation practice, and there is a teacher's guide with photocopyable activities.

Three of the stories in this reader are not supported with plays. These are the stories on Eleanor Roosevelt, Maya Ying Lin, and the Ordinary Citizen. If your students have been working with the other plays, they can be encouraged to work together to write and produce plays of their own based on these three stories.

Using both the plays and this reader, students will practice all their language skills, increase their vocabulary, and gain an appreciation for some of the most important issues and interesting individuals from American history.

User's Guide
for the student

The people in these stories did important things in the history of the United States at different times, in different places, and in different ways. Each of them worked hard on some problem or challenge that they and the country faced as it grew from thirteen English colonies on the east coast into a nation of fifty states with many millions of people from all the countries of the world.

These people faced great difficulties and in some cases danger, and they found ways to overcome them. In doing so, they made important contributions to history, and so we call them heroes. Their stories are real.

By reading these stories and doing the exercises, you will both learn some American history and improve your English. You will increase your vocabulary and practice speaking, listening, reading and writing.

Each unit in this book has thirteen parts:

- **Discuss**. Before reading, look at the picture and the map. Think and talk about what you already know about the hero. This will prepare you for the reading.

- **Read.** First read the short introduction. This will give you more information and some vocabulary that you will meet in the story.

- **Answer.** Working with a classmate, answer the first group of questions. Use information you learned in the discussion and the introductory reading. Now you are ready to read the story.

- **Read.** Read the story from beginning to end. Don't stop to look up any new words. Try to understand the words without your dictionary.

- **Answer These Questions.** After each story there are ten comprehension questions. Try to answer them without looking at the story. Don't worry if you can't answer all of them correctly. After you answer the questions, go back to the story to find the answers. This will help you understand the story better. Keep a record of your score on page 134. As you go through the stories, you will probably get more and more correct answers. This will show your progress.

- **Write.** Now that you have read the story, write short answers to the questions that you tried to answer before reading it (Discuss).

- **Timeline Scramble.** In this exercise you can use your understanding of the story by putting the events of the story in the correct order, from first to last. Go back to the story to check your answers. Do this alone or with a partner.

- **New Words.** Choose nine words from the story. Look for words that you don't know. Compare your list with your classmates' lists. Working together, choose several words that nobody knows. Ask your teacher to help you understand these words. Later you can look up the words on your list.

- **Working with Words.** This exercise will help you explore the different forms and uses of some of the words in the story.

- **Tell the Story.** Now tell the story to a partner without looking at it and listen as your partner tells the story, or you can each tell half of the story.

- **Test Yourself.** Read the story again. This time some of the words have been left out. From memory, write in the missing words. If you are not sure, guess. Then compare your answers with a partner's. If you disagree, go back to the story. Sometimes you may like your word better than the word in the story. Ask your teacher for an opinion. Perhaps you're right. By now you know the story very well.

- **Research and Write.** Write a paragraph or two about some topic in the story. Use an encyclopedia or another book or go to the internet for information.

- **What Does This Mean to You?** The heroes in these stories helped humanity in many different and important ways. What is your personal feeling about their accomplishment? A stamp or some other memento of the hero is shown. Is it meaningful to you? Express your feelings in a journal.

It is best to start with the first story and read the stories one after another. This will help you learn the history of the United States. In the 19th Century stories, there is a timeline for each story. On page 135 there is a 20th Century timeline. These timelines will help you connect the stories to each other. The final story, "The Ordinary Citizen," is a long summary that can be used as a review of all the heroes. There are several summary activities at the end of this story.

Heroes
from
American History

A Content-Based Reader

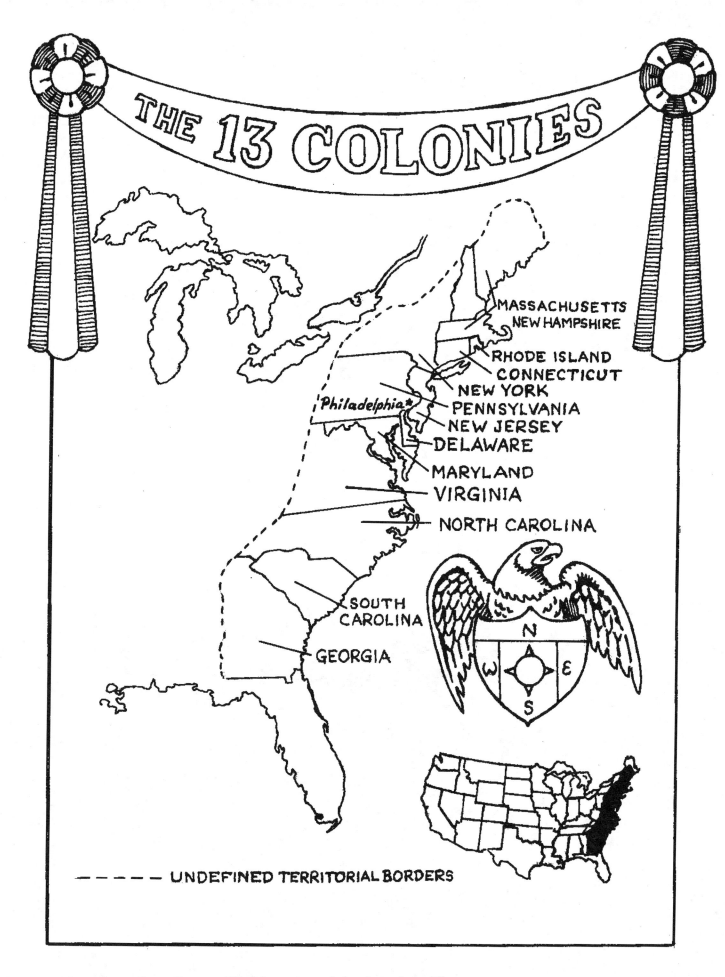

THE 13 COLONIES

MASSACHUSETTS
NEW HAMPSHIRE
RHODE ISLAND
CONNECTICUT
NEW YORK
Philadelphia*
PENNSYLVANIA
NEW JERSEY
DELAWARE
MARYLAND
VIRGINIA
NORTH CAROLINA
SOUTH CAROLINA
GEORGIA

N
W   E
S

— — — — — UNDEFINED TERRITORIAL BORDERS

Betsy Ross, George Washington, and the American Flag

Discuss

Look at the map and picture and share what you know about:

> The American flag
> George Washington
> The American Revolution
> Betsy Ross

Read

The time is 1776, and the American Revolutionary War has been going on for about a year. George Washington is general of the American army. The American colonies are fighting the British. The Americans want independence. They want to be a free country, but they have no flag. Washington asks Betsy Ross to make America's first flag.

Answer

1. What is going on in 1776?
2. How long has the war been going on?
3. Who is George Washington?
4. Who are the Americans fighting?
5. What do the Americans want?
6. What do the Americans need?
7. What does Washington ask Betsy Ross to do?

Read

Betsy Ross was born on January 1, 1752, in Philadelphia, Pennsylvania. She lived there all of her life. She married John Ross. The Ross family and George Washington went to the same church in Philadelphia.

Betsy Ross owned her own shop. She sewed covers for chairs and other pieces of furniture. She also sewed flags. Betsy made many flags for the Pennsylvania State Navy.

The American colonies wanted to be a free country. They were fighting the British, and they needed a new flag. During the early years of the American Revolution, Washington may have visited Betsy Ross in her home. There is no proof that this actually happened. There is no proof that it didn't happen. The story of Betsy Ross may be a legend. We do know that George Washington and Betsy Ross were both in Philadelphia at that time. It is believed that after Washington's visit, Betsy Ross made a flag for the new country.

On June 14, 1777, the American Congress did, in fact, accept a new flag for the thirteen colonies. It was called the Stars and Stripes. The congressional records described the flag of the thirteen United States: thirteen stripes, red and white, with thirteen white stars on a blue field. The colors of the flag have a special meaning. Red stands for courage, white for liberty, and blue for justice.

Some historians say that Betsy Ross did not make the first flag. But Betsy's grandson, William Canby, believed his grandmother did. In 1870, in a speech to the

Historical Society of Pennsylvania, he said that he remembered his grandmother talking about it. She told him about the meeting with George Washington.

Betsy died on January 30, 1836. Today a flag of the United States, still with thirteen stripes, but now with fifty stars, flies over her grave twenty-four hours a day. Her home is a historic landmark in Philadelphia. June 14 is celebrated as Flag Day in honor of America's first flag. On that day, many Americans fly the American flag at their homes.

Answer These Questions

Write T for true and F for false.

1. _____ Betsy Ross was born in New York.

2. _____ Betsy Ross owned a shop.

3. _____ Betsy Ross made flags for the British navy.

4. _____ George Washington may have visited Betsy Ross at her home.

5. _____ The American colonies needed a flag.

6. _____ There were thirteen colonies.

7. _____ The flag is called the stars and stripes.

8. _____ The first flag had thirteen stars.

9. _____ Betsy Ross died in 1936.

10. _____ Flag Day is in January.

Now go back to the story and check your answers. Write your score here and on page 134.

Number right _____/10

Write

Now what do you know about:

The American flag
George Washington
The American Revolution
Betsy Ross

Timeline Scramble

Finish the timeline.

1732 George Washington born

1752 _____

      _____

1775 *Revolution begins*

      _____

      _____

1777 _____

1799 George Washington dies

1836 _____

1870 _____

Today _____

1. Congress accepts flag
2. Washington visits Betsy
3. Betsy Ross born
4. Flag Day is June 14
5. Betsy Ross dies
6. Betsy marries John Ross
7. Canby gives speech
8. Betsy finishes flag
9. *Revolution begins*

Timeline

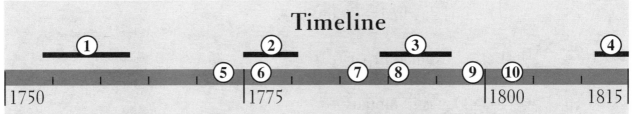

1. French and Indian War
2. American Revolution
3. Washington's Presidency
4. War of 1812
5. Boston Tea Party
6. Declaration of Independence
7. Constitution
8. Bill of Rights adopted
9. Washington dies
10. Louisiana Purchase

New Words

Look at the story again and underline nine words that you are not sure of.
Write them below and ask your classmates or teacher about them or look
them up in your dictionary.

_____   _____   _____

_____   _____   _____

_____   _____   _____

Working with Words

Make these words plural. Example: year   _years_

life   _____   colony   _____

family   _____   country   _____

church   _____   historian   _____

shop   _____   speech   _____

flag   _____   story   _____

Tell the Story of the First Flag

Use these words and phrases:

January 1, 1752   Stars and Stripes

Philadelphia, Pennsylvania   Betsy's grandson

John Ross   January 30, 1836

American Revolution   fifty stars

George Washington   historic landmark

Pennsylvania State Navy   June 14

June 14, 1777

Test Yourself

Read, write, and look again.

Betsy Ross was born on January 1, 1752, in Philadelphia, Pennsylvania. She lived there all of her _____. She married John Ross. The Ross family and George Washington went to the same _____ in Philadelphia.

Betsy Ross owned her own _____. She sewed covers for _____ and other pieces of furniture. She also sewed _____. Betsy made many flags for the Pennsylvania State Navy.

The American _____ wanted to be a free _____. They were fighting the British, and they needed a new flag. During the early years of the American Revolution, Washington may have _____ Betsy Ross in her home. There is no _____ that this actually happened. There is no proof that it didn't _____. The story of Betsy Ross may be a _____. We do know that George Washington and Betsy Ross were both in Philadelphia at that time. It is believed that after Washington's visit, Betsy Ross made a flag for the new country.

On June 14, 1777, the American Congress did, in fact, accept a new flag for the thirteen _____. It was called the Stars and _____. The congressional records described the flag of the thirteen United States: thirteen stripes, red and _____, with thirteen white stars on a _____ field. The colors of the flag have a special _____. Red stands for courage, white for liberty, and blue for justice.

Some _____ say that Betsy Ross did not make the first flag. But Betsy's _____, William Canby, believed his grandmother did. In 1870, in a _____ to the Historical Society of Pennsylvania, he said that he remembered his grandmother talking about it. She told him about the _____ with George Washington.

Betsy died on January 30, 1836. Today a flag of the United States, still with thirteen stripes, but now with _____ stars, flies over her _____ twenty-four hours a day. Her home is a historic landmark in Philadelphia. June 14 is _____ as Flag Day in honor of America's first flag. On that day, many Americans _____ the American flag at their homes.

Number correct _____ / 24. Put your score on page 134.

Research and Write

Find more information about the American flag and write a paragraph, or write a paragraph about your country's flag.

What Does This Mean to You?

Discuss the pledge or write about it in your journal.

Pledge of Allegiance to the Flag

I pledge allegiance to the flag of the United States of America and to the Republic for which it stands, one nation under God, indivisible, with liberty and justice for all.

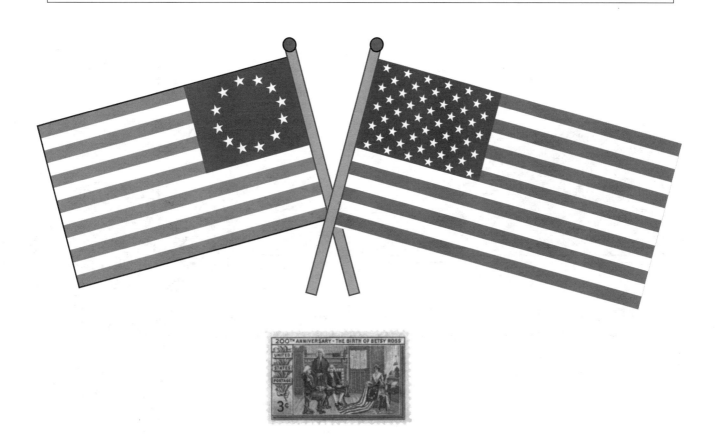

U.S. Post Office 1952

THE LEWIS AND CLARK EXPEDITION

OREGON COUNTRY

COLUMBIA RIVER

FORT CLATSOP

FORT MANDAN

MISSISSIPPI RIVER

MISSOURI RIVER

ROCKY MOUNTAINS

SPANISH TERRITORIES

LOUISIANA PURCHASE

INDIANA TERRITORY

ST. LOUIS

MISSISSIPPI RIVER

MISSISSIPPI TERRITORY

SPANISH FLORIDA

1804: THE AMERICAN WEST

━━━ WESTWARD ROUTE of the LEWIS & CLARK EXPEDITION

── BOUNDARIES of the LOUISIANA PURCHASE

- - - PRESENT DAY STATE BORDERS

∧∧∧ ROCKY MOUNTAINS

Sacagawea

Discuss

Look at the map and the picture and share what you know about:

Thomas Jefferson

The Louisiana Purchase

The Lewis and Clark Expedition

Sacagawea

Read

It is 1803, and Thomas Jefferson is the third president of the United States. The new nation has just bought a huge amount of land in the west. The land is called the Louisiana Purchase. It is wild, unknown, and dangerous. Jefferson wants to explore the land and find a way to the Pacific Ocean. He chooses two men for an expedition: Meriwether Lewis and William Clark. Their journey will begin in St. Louis in May, 1804. It will end at the Pacific Ocean in September, 1806. During the trip the explorers will meet a young Native American woman, Sacagawea. She became their guide and interpreter.

Answer

1. Who is Thomas Jefferson?
2. What does Jefferson want to do?
3. Who does Jefferson choose to lead an expedition?
4. Who will Lewis and Clark meet?
5. When will the expedition reach the Pacific Ocean?

Read

Sacagawea was a young Native American woman — perhaps eighteen years old — when she became an important part of the Lewis and Clark Expedition.

Sacagawea was a member of the Shoshone tribe. They lived in the Great Plains and the Rocky Mountains. One day an enemy tribe attacked Sacagawea's village, kidnapped her, and took her away. She was eleven years old. After that, she was sold to another tribe, and then to a fur trader named Charbonneau.

Sacagawea learned to survive during those terrible times, and she learned other Native American languages. In 1804, she and her husband, Charbonneau, came to Lewis and Clark's camp at Fort Mandan. The expedition was camping in a Native American village for the winter. Sacagawea was expecting a child in the spring.

Lewis and Clark knew that she would be a valuable addition to the expedition, and they asked her to join them. So, in the spring, after her son was born, Sacagawea, with a baby on her back, began the famous journey.

Her heroism and quick-thinking saved the expedition many times. One day a wind caused the boat she was in to fill with water. She quickly and calmly collected important documents and instruments that were floating away. Sacagawea saved almost everything.

At another time, the expedition needed strong horses to cross the dangerous Rocky Mountains. Without horses, the expedition would fail. Sacagawea guided them to a Shoshone village that she remembered from her childhood. That evening, William Clark asked her to be an interpreter at a meeting with the Shoshones. As she spoke, she recognized the chief. He was her own brother, Cameahwait! He gladly provided the expedition with horses.

Crossing the Rocky Mountains was not easy; the journey was long and dangerous. Often they were hungry, but Sacagawea was able to find enough food to keep them going.

Finally, the expedition reached the Pacific Ocean at Fort Clatsop on November 7, 1806. It was a success, thanks in part to this courageous young woman.

No one knows where or when she died. Most people believe it was in 1812 during an epidemic. William Clark raised and educated her little son who became a fine gentleman and helped others explore America.

Answer These Questions

Write T for true and F for false.

1. _____ Sacagawea was kidnapped by the Shoshone tribe.

2. _____ She learned other Native American languages.

3. _____ She was sold to a man named Charbonneau.

4. _____ Sacagawea's husband was an explorer.

5. _____ Sacagawea did not begin the trip with Lewis and Clark.

6. _____ The expedition needed boats to cross the Rocky Mountains.

7. _____ Sacagawea found her brother in a Shoshone village.

8. _____ The expedition took one year.

9. _____ Sacagawea died in the Rocky Mountains.

10. _____ William Clark raised and educated her son.

Now go back to the story and check your answers. Write your score here and on page 134.

Number right _____/10

Write

Now what do you know about:

Thomas Jefferson

The Louisiana Purchase

The Lewis and Clark Expedition

Sacagawea

Timeline Scramble

Finish the timeline.

1770 William Clark born

1774 Meriwether Lewis born

1787 *Sacagawea born*

_____

1803 _____

1804-May   The journey begins

1804-Winter _____

1805-Spring _____

_____

_____

1806 Expedition reaches the Pacific

1812 _____

_____

1. Sacagawea finds brother
2. Sacagaewa kidnapped
3. Clark raises her son
4. Sacagawea's son born
5. Sacagawea dies
6. *Sacagawea born*
7. Expedition crosses the Rocky Mountains
8. Louisiana Purchase
9. Sacagawea meets Lewis and Clark

Timeline

① ② ③ ④
⑤ ⑥ ⑦ ⑧ ⑨

1775   1800   1825   1850

1. Revolutionary War   4. Jackson's Presidency   7. Jefferson dies, July 4th
2. Jefferson's Presidency   5. Lewis & Clark head west   8. Clark dies
3. Jackson's Indian Wars   6. Lewis commits suicide   9. California Gold Rush

New Words

Look at the story again and underline nine words that you are not sure of. Write them below and ask your classmates or teacher about them or look them up in your dictionary.

_____   _____   _____

_____   _____   _____

_____   _____   _____

Working with Words

Choose the best word.

an _____ part of the expedition	courageous
during these _____ times	strong
a _____ addition to the expedition	*easy*
began the _____ journey	valuable
needed _____ horses	important
crossing the Rocky Mountains was not _easy_	young
the journey was _____ and _____	fine
Often they were _____	terrible
this _____ young woman	famous
her _____ son	hungry
a _____ gentleman	long, dangerous

Tell the Story of Sacagawea

Use these words and phrases:

eighteen years old	horses
member of the Shoshone tribe	Cameahwait
kidnapped	Rocky Mountains
Charbonneau	Pacific Ocean
Lewis and Clark's camp	epidemic
baby	William Clark

Test Yourself

Read, write, and look again.

Sacagawea was a young Native American woman — perhaps eighteen years old — when she became an important part of the Lewis and Clark _____.

Sacagawea was a member of the Shoshone _____. They lived in the Great Plains and the Rocky Mountains. One day an enemy tribe _____ Sacagawea's village, kidnapped her, and took her away. She was eleven years old. After that, she was sold to another _____, and then to a fur trader named Charbonneau.

Sacagawea learned to _____ during those terrible times, and she learned other Native American _____. In 1804, she and her husband, Charbonneau, came to Lewis and Clark's camp at Fort Mandan. The expedition was _____ in a Native American village for the winter. Sacagawea was expecting a _____ in the spring.

Lewis and Clark knew that she would be a valuable addition to the expedition, and they asked her to _____ them. So, in the spring, after her son was born, Sacagawea, with a baby on her _____, began the famous journey.

Her heroism and quick-thinking saved the _____ many times. One day a wind caused the boat she was in to _____ with water. She quickly and calmly collected important _____ and instruments that were floating away. Sacagawea saved almost everything.

At another time, the expedition needed strong _____ to cross the danger-ous Rocky Mountains. Without horses, the expedition would _____. Sacagawea guided them to a Shoshone village that she remembered from her childhood. That evening, William Clark asked her to be an _____ at a meeting with the Shoshones. As she spoke, she recognized the chief. He was her own brother, Cameahwait! He gladly _____ the expedition with horses.

Crossing the Rocky Mountains was not easy; the journey was long and _____. Often they were _____, but Sacagawea was able to find enough food to keep them going.

Finally, the expedition _____ the Pacific Ocean at Fort Clatsop on November 7, 1806. It was a _____, thanks in part to this _____ young woman.

No one knows where or when she died. Most people believe it was in 1812 during an _____. William Clark raised and educated her little _____ who became a fine gentleman and helped others _____ America.

Number correct _____ **/25.** Put your score on page 134.

Research and Write

Find more information and write a paragraph about one of these topics:
(A) Thomas Jefferson, (B) the Louisiana Purchase, (C) Shoshone Indians,
(D) the Rocky Mountains.

What Do These Mean to You?

Discuss these coins and stamps or write about them in your journal.

U.S. Mint 2000
U.S. Post Office 1948

1895 Indian Head penny, 1998 Red Cloud stamp, 1936 Indian Head nickel

What Do These Places Have in Common?

What does this suggest about the history of the United States? Is this important to the present and the future? Write about your ideas and feelings in your journal.

Chicopee, Massachusetts
Naugatuck, Connecticut
Saginaw, Michigan
Chattanooga, Tennessee
Chicago, Illinois
Wichita, Kansas
Omaha, Nebraska

Natchez, Mississippi
Mankato, Minnesota
Sioux Falls, South Dakota
Muskogee, Oklahoma
Cheyenne, Wyoming
Klamath Falls, Oregon
Kodiak, Alaska

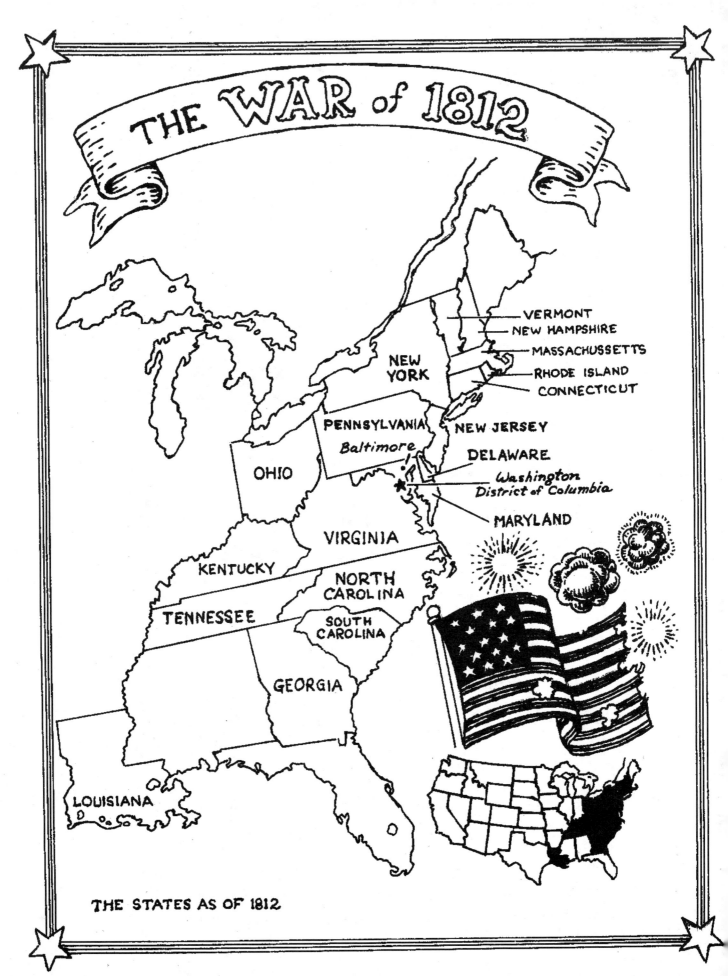

THE WAR of 1812

VERMONT
NEW HAMPSHIRE
MASSACHUSSETTS
RHODE ISLAND
CONNECTICUT

NEW YORK

PENNSYLVANIA
Baltimore

NEW JERSEY

DELAWARE

*Washington
District of Columbia*

OHIO

MARYLAND

VIRGINIA

KENTUCKY

NORTH
CAROLINA

TENNESSEE

SOUTH
CAROLINA

GEORGIA

LOUISIANA

THE STATES AS OF 1812

Dolley Madison

Read

The date is August 23, 1814. The Americans and the British are at war again. The British are invading Washington, D.C. This is the War of 1812. Dolley Madison is the wife of the fourth president of the United States, James Madison. She is called the First Lady. She is alone in the president's house. She is in danger, but she bravely saves George Washington's portrait and many important documents. She escapes just before the British burn the house.

Answer

1. What is going on in 1814?
2. Who is James Madison?
3. Where is Dolley Madison on August 23?
4. What are the British doing?
5. What does Dolley Madison do?

Read

Dolley Madison was born on May 20, 1768, in North Carolina. Later, she moved to Philadelpia. There she met and married John Todd, a lawyer. They had two sons.

In August, 1793, there was an epidemic of yellow fever in Philadelphia. Both her husband and her second son died. She became a widow with a young child to care for. Soon after that she met and married James Madison, who later became president in 1809.

As James Madison's wife, she became America's First Lady. Dolley's good manners and her beauty made her a very popular First Lady in America. She entertained foreign visitors with style.

However, it was one simple act of courage for which she will always be remembered. After the American Revolutionary War, the Americans and the British were fighting once again. It was called the War of 1812. The Americans were protesting British trade policies.

On August 23, 1814, Dolley Madison was alone in the president's house. The president was away. She learned that the British were invading the capital, but she refused to leave. She insisted on staying until valuable documents and the portrait of George Washington were packed — even though she was in great danger.

In fact, the British were nearly on her doorstep — she could hear the cannons in the distance. She left just in time. The British enterd the house, ate the food, drank the wine and burned the house.

Of course, after the war was over, the house had to be restored. It was painted white to cover the burn marks. Slowly, people began calling the president's home the White House. Then, in 1902, President Theodore Roosevelt made it official. The president's home was named The White House.

After leaving office, the Madisons retired to their estate in Virginia where James Madison died in 1836. Dolley then returned to Washington where she was welcomed as a national hero. The nation thanked her for her special role as First Lady and a brave patriot. She died on July 12, 1849, at the age of 81.

Answer These Questions

Write T for true and F for false.

1. _____ Dolley Madison was born in Virginia.

2. _____ Dolley Madison's first husband died in the war.

3. _____ She became a widow with two small children.

4. _____ James Madison was America's second president.

5. _____ Dolley Madison was beautiful.

6. _____ The American and British were fighting about British trade policies.

7. _____ The British invaded Washington, D.C.

8. _____ Dolley Madison saved George Washington.

9. _____ The British burned the Madison's home.

10. _____ The president's house is now called The White House.

Now go back to the story and check your answers. Write your score here and on page 134.

Number right _____/10

Write

Now what do you know about:

James Madison
The White House
The War of 1812
Dolley Madison

Timeline Scramble

Finish the timeline.

1768	*Dolley is born*
1793	_____
	_____
1809	_____
1812	War with Britain begins
	_____
	_____
1836	James Madison dies
	_____
1849	_____
1902	_____

1. Marries James Madison
2. Dolley dies
3. Dolley returns to Washington
4. John Todd dies
5. Becomes First Lady
6. *Dolley is born*
7. Roosevelt names White House
8. British burn White House
9. White House restored

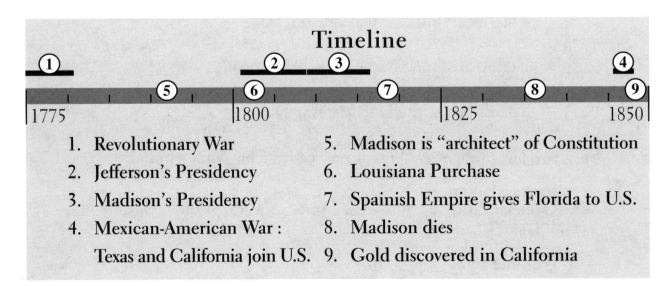

Timeline

1775   1800   1825   1850

1. Revolutionary War
2. Jefferson's Presidency
3. Madison's Presidency
4. Mexican-American War :
   Texas and California join U.S.
5. Madison is "architect" of Constitution
6. Louisiana Purchase
7. Spanish Empire gives Florida to U.S.
8. Madison dies
9. Gold discovered in California

New Words

Look at the story again and underline nine words that you are not sure of. Write them below and ask your classmates or teacher about them or look them up in your dictionary.

_____   _____   _____

_____   _____   _____

_____   _____   _____

Working with Words

There is a verb in each of these nouns. Write the verb beside the noun.

Example: Meeting   _meet_

Noun	Verb	Noun	Verb
movement	_____	restoration	_____
marriage	_____	covering	_____
entertainment	_____	retirement	_____
invasion	_____	insistence	_____
refusal	_____	entrance	_____

Tell the Story of Dolley Madison

Use these words and phrases:

May 20, 1768	August 23, 1814
North Carolina	invading
Philadelphia	documents
yellow fever	burned
James Madison	retired
First Lady	returned
the War of 1812	July 12, 1849

Test Yourself

Read, write, and look again.

Dolley Madison was born on May 20, 1768, in North Carolina. later, she _____ to Philadelpia. There she met and married John Todd, a lawyer. They had two _____.

In August, 1793, there was an epidemic of yellow fever in _____. Both her husband and her second son died. She became a widow with a young child to care for. Soon after that she _____ and married James Madison, who later became president in 1809.

As James Madison's wife, she became America's First _____. Dolley's good manners and her _____ made her a very _____ First Lady in America. She entertained foreign _____ with style.

However, it was one simple act of _____ for which she will always be remembered. After the American Revolutionary War, the Americans and the British were _____ once again. It was called the War of 1812. The Americans were _____ British trade policies.

On August 23, 1814, Dolley Madison was _____ in the president's house. The president was away. She learned that the British were _____ the capital, but she refused to leave. She insisted on staying until valuable _____ and the portrait of George Washington were packed — even though she was in great _____.

In fact, the British were _____ on her doorstep — she could hear the _____ in the distance. She left just ___ _____. The British entered the house, ate the food, drank the wine and _____ the house.

Of course, after the war was _____, the house had to be restored. It was painted white to _____ the burn marks. Slowly, people began calling the president's home the White House. Then, in 1902, President Theodore Roosevelt made it _____. The president's home was _____ The White House.

After leaving office, the Madisons _____ to their estate in Virginia where James Madison died in 1836. Dolley then _____ to Washington where she was welcomed as a national _____. The nation _____ her for her special role as First Lady and a brave patriot. She died on July 12, 1849, at the _____ of 81.

Number correct _____/29. Put your score on page 134.

Research and Write

Find more information and write a paragraph about one of these topics:
(A) the War of 1812, (B) the White House, or (C)James Madison.

What Does This Mean to You?

Discuss this letter or write about it in your journal.

from Dolley Madison's letter to her sister, August 23, 1814

Three o'clock. — Will you believe it, my sister? We have had a battle . . . near Bladensburg, and here I am still, within sound of the cannon! Mr. Madison comes not. May God protect us! Two messengers, covered with dust, come to bid me fly; but here I mean to wait for him . . . At this late hour a wagon has been procured, and I have had it filled with plate and the most valuable portable articles, belonging to the house. Whether it will reach its destination, the "Bank of Maryland," or fall into the hands of the British soldiery, events must determine. Our kind friend, Mr. Carroll, has come to hasten my departure, and is in a very bad humor with me, because I insist on waiting until the large picture of General Washington is secured . . . It is done! and the precious portrait placed in the hands of two gentlemen of New York for safe keeping. And now, dear sister, I must leave this house, . . .

U.S. Post Office 1981

SLAVERY in 1850

BOSTON
HARTFORD, CT
LITCHFIELD, CT
OHIO
CINCINNATI

☐ Free States and Territories

■ Slave States and Territories

Harriet Beecher Stowe

Discuss

Look at the map and the picture and share what you know about:

The American Civil War

Slavery in the United States

Uncle Tom's Cabin and Harriet Beecher Stowe

The Emancipation Proclamation

Read

The year is 1852. The country is deeply divided on the issue of slavery. The northern states are against it. They say it is wrong. The southern states are for it. They say they need slaves to work on their plantations. A new book is published. It is *Uncle Tom's Cabin* by Harriet Beecher Stowe. It is an anti-slavery book, and it helps to change history. In 1861, the North and the South will go to war — The American Civil War.

Answer

1. What issue divides the North and the South?
2. Why does the South need slavery?
3. What happens in 1852?
4. What does *Uncle Tom's Cabin* do?
5. What will happen in 1861?

Read

Harriet Beecher Stowe was born in Litchfield, Connecticut on June 14, 1811. She was one of eleven children. In 1832, the family moved to Cincinnati, Ohio, where she met and married Calvin Stowe. They had seven children and very little money. Harriet began writing for a magazine to help pay the bills.

During this time Harriet saw the slave trade firsthand. Although Ohio was a northern state without slavery, slave trading was very common across the river in Kentucky, a southern state. Slaves were bought and sold there. Harriet was horrified, and that is probably how she got the idea for an anti-slavery book.

Uncle Tom's Cabin first appeared as a serial in a newspaper — each week a new chapter was published. It was an exciting story. Readers were eager to get the next issue. They wanted to know what happened to Eliza, the runaway slave.

The complete book was published in 1852. It immediately became a best seller. It ignited strong feelings about slavery. Until that time, people did not have a clear picture of this horrible practice. Now they became very angry about how Negroes were treated. Wasn't this a free country? Weren't all people equal? Wasn't slavery very wrong? The book further divided the North and the South. Some say it even led to the American Civil War.

In fact, when Harriet visited President Lincoln at the White House, he said, "So you're the little woman who started the big war." Harriet had come to the White House to encourage Lincoln to sign the Emancipation Proclamation. This was a document that said all Negroes were free.

On January 1, 1863, President Lincoln signed the proclamation. Harriet was at a concert in Boston on that day. At intermission the signing of the Emancipation Proclamation was announced. The crowd went wild. Then they remembered that Harriet was there. Immediately, the crowd began chanting and cheering for her. She smiled and bowed. It was a night to remember.

In her last years, Harriet began traveling and making speeches. She was now famous and had many friends. On July 1, 1896, at the age of 82, she died in Hartford, Connecticut. Her book, *Uncle Tom's Cabin*, had become famous around the world.

Answer These Questions

Write T for true and F for false.

1. _____ Harriet Beecher Stowe was born in Ohio.

2. _____ She had eleven children.

3. _____ Harriet lived in a slave state.

4. _____ *Uncle Tom's Cabin* was an immediate success.

5. _____ The book was a best seller.

6. _____ Harriet visited Abraham Lincoln in the White House.

7. _____ She wanted Lincoln to sign the Emancipation Proclamation.

8. _____ The Emancipation Proclamation gave Negroes freedom.

9. _____ Harriet was at home when the Proclamation was announced.

10. _____ In her last years, Harriet stopped traveling.

Now go back to the story and check your answers. Write your score here and on page 134.

   Number right _____/10

Write

Now what do you know about:

The American Civil War
Slavery in the United States
Uncle Tom's Cabin
　　and Harriet Beecher Stowe
The Emancipation Proclamation

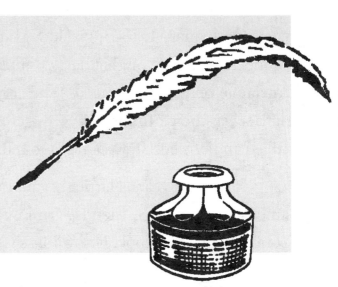

Timeline Scramble

Finish the timeline.

1811 ＿＿＿＿＿＿＿＿＿＿＿＿＿＿

1832 ＿＿＿＿＿＿＿＿＿＿＿＿＿＿

＿＿＿＿＿＿＿＿＿＿＿＿＿＿

＿＿＿＿＿＿＿＿＿＿＿＿＿＿

1852 ＿＿＿＿＿＿＿＿＿＿＿＿＿＿

1861 ＿＿＿＿＿＿＿＿＿＿＿＿＿＿

1862 *Harriet meets Lincoln*

1863 ＿＿＿＿＿＿＿＿＿＿＿＿＿＿

＿＿＿＿＿＿＿＿＿＿＿＿＿＿

1896 ＿＿＿＿＿＿＿＿＿＿＿＿＿＿

1. Marries Calvin Stowe
2. Harriet travels and gives speeches
3. Civil War begins
4. Harriet moves to Cincinnati
5. Harriet dies
6. *Harriet meets Lincoln*
7. "Uncle Tom's Cabin" appears in newspaper
8. "Uncle Tom's Cabin" published as book
9. Harriet Beecher Stowe born
10. Emancipation Proclamation signed

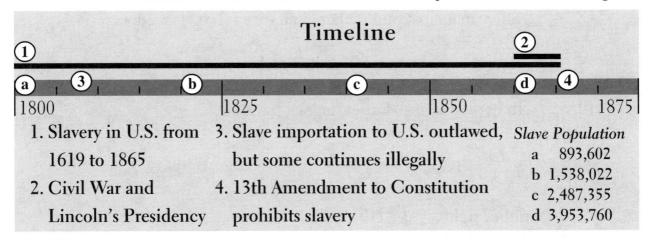

Timeline

1. Slavery in U.S. from 1619 to 1865
2. Civil War and Lincoln's Presidency
3. Slave importation to U.S. outlawed, but some continues illegally
4. 13th Amendment to Constitution prohibits slavery

Slave Population
a　　893,602
b 1,538,022
c 2,487,355
d 3,953,760

New Words

Look at the story again and underline nine words that you are not sure of. Write them below and ask your classmates or teacher about them or look them up in your dictionary.

_____   _____   _____

_____   _____   _____

_____   _____   _____

Working with Words

Put these verbs in the past tense.

Example: She moves   _She moved_

marries   _____   starts   _____

appears   _____   signs   _____

wants   _____   remembers   _____

happens   _____   chants   _____

ignites   _____   cheers   _____

treats   _____   smiles   _____

divides   _____   bows   _____

visits   _____   dies   _____

Tell the Story of Harriet Beecher Stowe

Use these words and phrases:

June 14, 1811	_Uncle Tom's Cabin_
Litchfield, Connecticut	1852
Cincinnati, Ohio	American Civil War
1832	Abraham Lincoln
seven children	Emancipation Proclamation
slave trade	July 1, 1896
Kentucky	Hartford, Connecticut

Test Yourself

Read, write, and look again.

Harriet Beecher Stowe was _____ in Litchfield, Connecticut on June 14, 1811. She was ____ of eleven children. In 1832, the family moved to Cincinnati, Ohio, where she met and _____ Calvin Stowe. They had seven children and very little _____. Harriet began writing for a _____ to help pay the bills.

During this time Harriet saw the slave _____ firsthand. Although Ohio was a northern state without _____, slave trading was very common across the river in Kentucky, a southern state. Slaves were _____ and sold there. Harriet was horrified, and that is probably how she got the _____ for an anti-slavery book.

Uncle Tom's Cabin first _____ as a serial in a _____ — each week a new chapter was published. It was an exciting _____. Readers were eager to get the next _____. They wanted to know what happened to Eliza, the runaway _____.

The complete book was _____ in 1852. It immediately became a best seller. It ignited _____ feelings about slavery. Until that time, people did not have a clear picture of this _____ practice. Now they became very _____ about how Negroes were _____. Wasn't this a free _____? Weren't all people equal? Wasn't _____ very wrong? The book further divided the North and the South. Some say it even led to the American Civil War.

In fact, when Harriet _____ President Lincoln at the White House, he said, "So you're the little _____ who started the big _____." Harriet had come to the White House to encourage Lincoln to _____ the Emancipation Proclamation. This was a _____ that said all Negroes were free.

On January 1, 1863, President Lincoln _____ the proclamation. Harriet was at a _____ in Boston on that day. At intermission the _____ of the Emancipation Proclamation was announced. The crowd went wild. Then they remembered that Harriet was _____. Immediately, the crowd began chanting and cheering for her. She smiled and bowed. It was a _____ to remember.

In her last years, Harriet began traveling and making _____. She was now _____ and had many friends. On July 1, 1896, at the age of 82, she _____ in Hartford, Connecticut. Her book, *Uncle Tom's Cabin*, had become famous around the _____.

Number correct _____/25. Put your score on page 134.

Research and Write

Find more information and write a paragraph about one of these topics: (A) The Civil War, (B) the slave trade, (C) the Emancipation Proclamation, or (D) *Uncle Tom's Cabin*.

What Does This Mean to You?

Discuss this article from the Associated Press, Friday, January 18, 2002, or write about it in your journal.

Serial of Stowe Classic Donated to College

BRUNSWICK, Maine (AP)– While rummaging through the attic of a 300-year-old home, Jack Conway of Attleboro, Mass., found old newspapers that had published *"Uncle Tom's Cabin"* as a serial before the classic novel came out as a book.

Now, the newspaper copies are being donated to Bowdoin College, and officials at the private school in Brunswick are thrilled.

"It's such an important book in American History and for Bowdoin because (Harriet Beecher Stowe) wrote it here," said Richard Lindemann, director of special collections and archives at the college.

Stowe's husband, Calvin, was a religion professor at Bowdoin in 1852, the year *"Uncle Tom's Cabin"* was published.

A contractor noticed the newspapers while inspecting a Massachusetts house Conway and his wife plan to buy and renovate.

Conway did not say where the house is located.

As a historian who's written a book on American classics, Conway knew Stowe's anti-slavery book appeared in serial form in 1851 and 1852 in *The National Era,* an abolitionist newspaper published in Washington, D.C., and Bowdoin's collection extended only through the December 1851 issue.

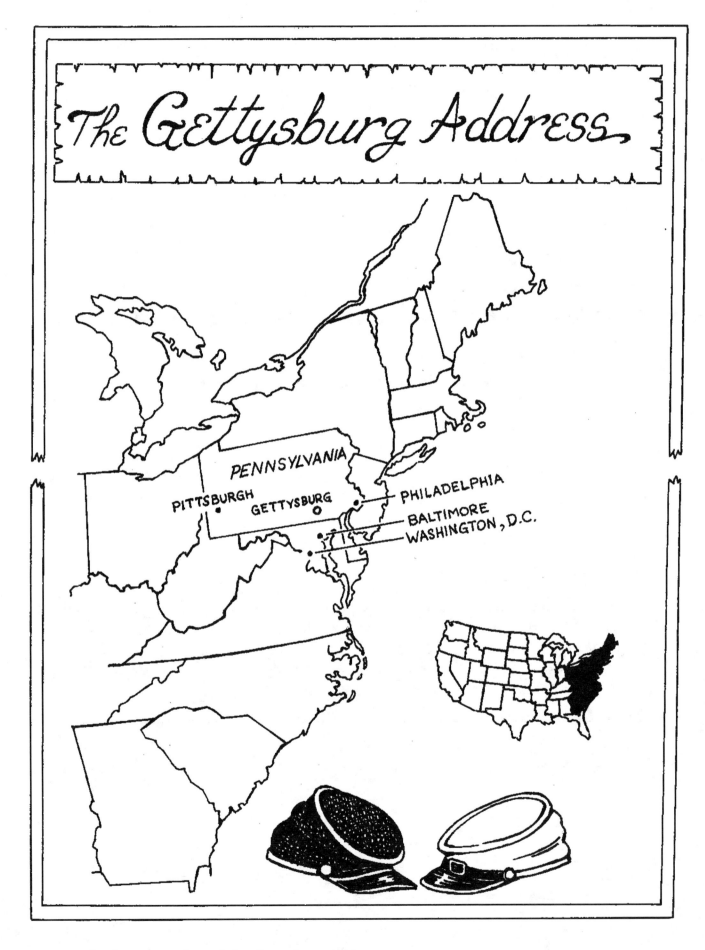

The Gettysburg Address

PENNSYLVANIA

PITTSBURGH • GETTYSBURG ○ — PHILADELPHIA

BALTIMORE
WASHINGTON, D.C.

Abraham Lincoln and the Gettysburg Address

Discuss

Look at the map and the picture and share what you know about:

The American Civil War

Abraham Lincoln

The Battle of Gettysburg

The Gettysburg Address

Read

The year is 1863. The Civil War has been going on for three years. The war is between the northern and southern states. One battle, the Battle of Gettysburg, in Pennsylvania, has been especially bloody. Fifty thousand soldiers lie dead. People are tired of the war, and want peace. President Lincoln comes to the Gettysburg battlefield to give a speech to honor the dead and to unite the nation. It will be one of the most famous speeches in history.

Answer

1. What has been going on since 1863?
2. Where is Gettysburg?
3. What happened there?
4. How do people feel?
5. Why does Lincoln come to Gettysburg?
6. Describe Lincoln's speech.

Read

President Abraham Lincoln almost didn't make one of the most famous speeches in history, the Gettysburg address at the Gettysburg battlefield. He was invited just a few weeks before the ceremony, and many people thought he would not come because another man, Edward Everett, was to be the main speaker. Everett was an excellent speaker. He had a deep, rich voice, and people loved to listen to him.

However, Lincoln accepted the invitation. He knew his presence and what he said would be important. People were tired of war. They didn't care if the union would survive or not, and they didn't care if the United States would be one nation or two. And they didn't care about slavery anymore. They just wanted the war to be over.

Lincoln put a lot of thought into the speech because he knew people were discouraged. He wanted to remind people that this country was a free country and that all men were created equal. This was an important time for America.

The big day came. Thousands of people came. The guests marched into the battlefield. Lincoln rode on a horse. A mother asked the president if her three-year old daughter could ride with him because she was so tired. The president didn't mind at all, and the little girl rode with him.

There were many speeches that day. Finally, Lincoln read his short speech. There was no applause and no cheering after he finished. Most people didn't realize that they had listened to one of the greatest speeches in history. Lincoln thought he had failed. Edward Everett thought it was a wonderful speech. He told the president it took him two hours to say what the president said in two minutes.

Today, many schoolchildren memorize the Gettysburg Address. Lincoln's words have become famous: ". . . that this nation under God, shall have a new birth of freedom — and that government of the people, by the people, for the people, shall not perish from the earth."

Answer These Questions

Write T for true and F for false.

1. _____ President Lincoln almost didn't make his famous speech.

2. _____ Everybody expected Lincoln to come.

3. _____ Lincoln was not the main speaker.

4. _____ The people were tired of war.

5. _____ Lincoln rode on a horse to the battlefield.

6. _____ Everybody applauded when Lincoln finished.

7. _____ Edward Everett liked Lincoln's speech.

8. _____ Lincoln thought his speech was a failure.

9. _____ Lincoln's speech was only two minutes long.

10. _____ Today all children must memorize the Gettysburg address.

Now go back to the story and check your answers. Write your score here and on page 134.

Number right _____/10

Write

Now what do you know about:

The American Civil War
Abraham Lincoln
The Battle of Gettysburg
The Gettysburg Address

Timeline Scramble

Finish the timeline.

1809	Abraham Lincoln born	1. Lincoln gives address
1861	_____	2. Lincoln prepares address
1863	_____	3. Lincoln rides to battlefield
	_____	4. Civil War begins
	Lincoln accepts invitation	5. Children memorize address
	_____	6. Gettysburg battle
	_____	7. *Lincoln accepts invitation*
	_____	8. Lincoln invited to speak
1865	Civil War ends	
	_____	

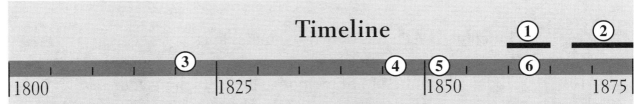

Timeline

1. Civil War and Lincoln's Presidency
2. Radical Reconstruction punishes the South
3. Missouri Compromise balances slave and free states.
4. Mexican War; U.S. takes the West including Texas and California
5. Balance of slave/free states lost with Kansas/Nebraska Act; fighting begins
6. War ends, Lincoln assassinated

New Words

Look at the story again and underline nine words that you are not sure of. Write them below and ask your classmates or teacher about them or look them up in your dictionary.

_____	_____	_____
_____	_____	_____
_____	_____	_____

Working with Words

Make these phrases positive. Example: he didn't make _____he made_____

they didn't think   _____
they didn't invite   _____
they didn't love   _____
he didn't accept   _____
he didn't know   _____
they didn't want   _____
they didn't care   _____
he didn't put   _____
the day didn't come   _____
thousands didn't come   _____
he didn't ride   _____
they didn't realize   _____
he didn't think   _____
he didn't tell   _____
they don't memorize   _____

Tell the Story of Lincoln's Gettysburg Address

Use these words and phrases:

Gettysburg battle   many speeches
invited   no applause
Edward Everett   failed
Lincoln accepted   Edward Everett
tired of war   memorize
thousands came   of. . . by. . . for . . .
rode   perish

Test Yourself

Read, write, and look again.

President Abraham Lincoln almost didn't make one of the most _____ speeches in history, the Gettysburg address at the Gettysburg _____. He was _____ just a few weeks before the ceremony, and many people thought he would not _____ because another man, Edward Everett, was to be the main _____. Everett was an excellent speaker. He had a deep, rich _____, and people loved to _____ to him.

However, Lincoln _____ the invitation. He knew his presence and what he said would be _____. People were tired of _____. They didn't care _____ the union would _____ or not, and they didn't care if the United States would be one nation or _____. And they didn't care about _____ anymore. They just wanted the war to be _____.

Lincoln put a lot of _____ into the speech because he _____ people were discouraged. He wanted to remind people that this country was a _____ country and that all men were created _____. This was an _____ time for America.

The big day came. _____ of people came. The guests marched onto the _____. Lincoln _____ on a horse. A mother asked the president if her three-year old daughter could _____ with him because she was so _____. The president didn't mind at all, and the little girl rode _____ him.

There were many _____ that day. Finally, Lincoln read his _____ speech. There was no _____ and no cheering after he _____. Most people didn't _____ that they had listened to one of the greatest speeches in _____. Lincoln thought he had _____. Edward Everett thought it was a _____ speech. He told the president it took him two _____ to say what the president said in two _____.

Today, many schoolchildren _____ the Gettysburg Address. Lincoln's _____ have become famous: ". . . that this _____ under God, shall have a new birth of freedom — and that government ____ the people, ____ the people, _____ the people, shall not perish from the _____."

Number correct _____ **/25.** Put your score on page 134.

Research and Write

Find more information and write a paragraph about one of these topics: (A) The Civil War, (B) the Battle of Gettysburg, (C) Abraham Lincoln.

What Does This Speech Mean to You?

Discuss the Gettysburg Address or write about it in your journal.

The Gettysburg Address

Four score and seven years ago our fathers brought forth on this continent, a new nation, conceived in Liberty, and dedicated to the proposition that all men are created equal.

Now we are engaged in a great civil war, testing whether that nation, or any nation so conceived and so dedicated, can long endure. We are met on a great battlefield of that war. We have come to dedicate a portion of that field, as the final resting place for those who here gave their lives that that nation might live. It is altogether fitting and proper that we should do this.

But, in a larger sense, we can not dedicate — we can not consecrate — we can not hallow — this ground. The brave men, living and dead, who struggled here, have consecrated it, far above our poor power to add or detract. The world will little note, nor long remember what we say here, but it can never forget what they did here. It is for us the living, rather, to be dedicated here to the unfinished work which they who fought here have thus far so nobly advanced. It is rather for us to be here dedicated to the great task remaining before us — that from these honored dead we take increased devotion to that cause for which they gave the last full measure of devotion — that we here highly resolve that these dead shall not have died in vain — that this nation, under God, shall have a new birth of freedom — and that government of the people, by the people, for the people, shall not perish from the earth.

November 19, 1863

U.S. Post Office 1948

Thomas A. Edison

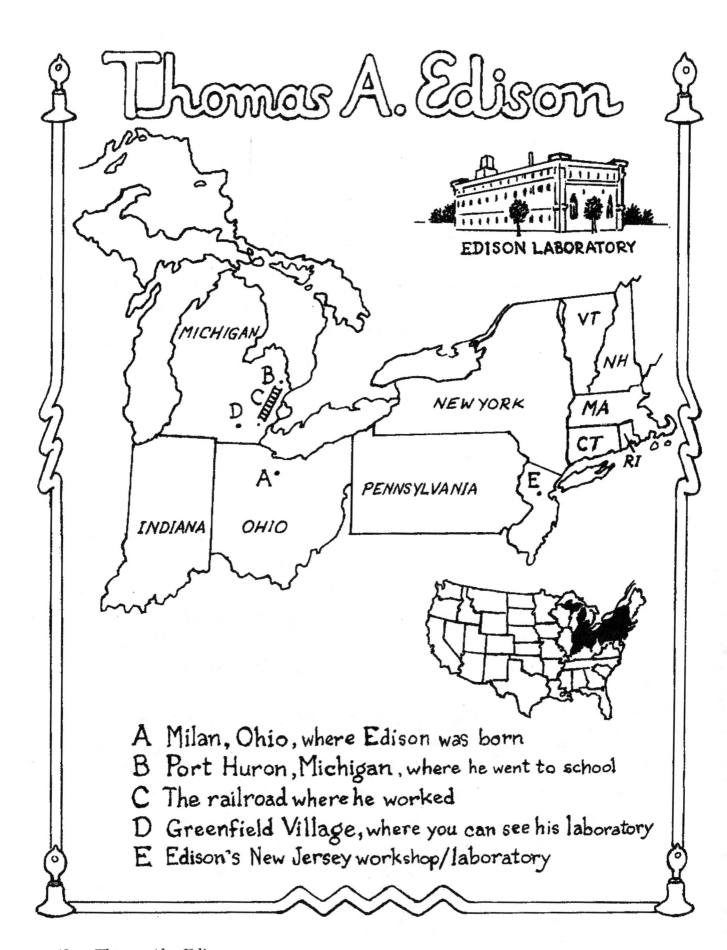

EDISON LABORATORY

A Milan, Ohio, where Edison was born
B Port Huron, Michigan, where he went to school
C The railroad where he worked
D Greenfield Village, where you can see his laboratory
E Edison's New Jersey workshop/laboratory

Thomas Alva Edison

Discuss

Look at the map and the picture and share what you know about:

Thomas Edison

The telegraph

Edison's inventions: The electric light bulb

The phonograph

The motion picture camera

Read

Thomas Edison was a world-famous inventor. He made over 1000 inventions, more than any other man in history. The electric light bulb, the phonograph, and the motion picture camera are just a few of his many inventions. Although he became deaf, he continued to make inventions. He never went to college or even school; he was taught by his mother and by himself. His contribution to people everywhere is amazing.

Answer

1. Who was Thomas Edison?
2. How many inventions did he make?
3. Name three of his inventions.
4. Describe his education.

Read

Thomas Edison was born on February 11, 1847, in Milan, Ohio. He was the youngest of seven children in his family. It was clear from the beginning that Thomas was curious about everything. He wanted to know the "why" and "how" of everything. Why does water put out fire? How do birds fly? Why and how and why?

His school teacher had no time or patience for such questions. In fact, he told Thomas' mother that there was something wrong with Thomas' brain. Thomas asked too many questions. He was too hard to control.

His mother was shocked and angry; she knew he was a smart boy. She took him out of school and decided to teach him herself. From then on, Thomas never went to school and learned only what he wanted to — and he wanted to learn everything. For example, a chemistry book his mother bought him interested him very much. He did every experiment in the book.

The public library was also his teacher. He started at one end of the bookshelf and read every book on it. Then he began another.

When he was fourteen, he saved the life of a child from an on-coming train. The child's father was so grateful that he gave Thomas a job in his telegraph office. There he learned about sending messages by wire, and he even improved the process.

At that time, he began to lose his hearing, and by the time he was an adult, he was almost totally deaf. This did not stop him from working or inventing. He did not consider his problem a tragedy, and failure never discouraged him. Yet, he didn't think of himself as a genius. He once said, "Genius is one percent inspiration and ninety-nine percent perspiration."

In 1876, he built a science laboratory in Menlo Park, New Jersey. Work was his first love; family and friends came second. He enjoyed working so much that he had little time to sleep. When he was tired, he took short naps. He even had a cot in his laboratory.

He was celebrated all over the world for his inventions. He is probably best known for the electric light bulb, the phonograph, and the motion picture camera, but he worked on hundreds of projects. He set up the world's first electric power station in New York. His discoveries in electronics later led to such things as the radio, x-ray machines, and computers.

He died at the age of eighty-four, on October 18, 1931. That night, the nation turned out its lights in honor of this genius who made their lives so much better. He turned night into day.

Answer These Questions

Write T for true and F for false.

1. _____ Thomas Edison had several brothers and sisters.

2. _____ His school teacher loved Thomas' curiosity.

3. _____ Thomas' mother was a school teacher.

4. _____ He did not go to college.

5. _____ He worked in a telephone office.

6. _____ Thomas began to lose his eyesight.

7. _____ Sometimes he slept in his laboratory.

8. _____ He invented the telegraph.

9. _____ He died when he was still very young.

10. _____ On the night he died, people turned off their lights.

Now go back to the story and check your answers. Write your score here and on page 134.

Number right _____/10

Write

Now what do you know about:

Thomas Edison
The telegraph
Edison's inventions: The electric light bulb
The phonograph
The motion picture camera

Timeline Scramble

Finish the timeline.

1847 _____

_____

Mother teaches him

1851 _____

_____

_____

1876 _____

1879   invents light bulb

1931 _____

_____

1. Builds a lab in New Jersey
2. Edison dies
3. Saves child's life
4. Loses hearing
5. *Mother teaches him*
6. Works in telegraph office
7. Edison born
8. Nation turns out lights
9. Trouble with teacher

Timeline

Each of the earlier units in this book has told the story of an American hero who lived in the 18th or 19th Century. In each unit there was a timeline showing the relationship of their activities with other events during their time. The people in this and following stories may have been born in the 19th Century, but the impact of their lives was primarily on the 20th Century. At the back of the book on page 135 there is a 20th Century timeline, which will help you connect the stories to each other.

New Words

Look at the story again and underline nine words that you are not sure of. Write them below and ask your classmates or teacher about them or look them up in your dictionary.

_____   _____   _____

_____   _____   _____

_____   _____   _____

Working with Words

Use one of these prepositions in the phrases below.

on   **of**   **in**   **from**   **at**

1. born _____ February, 11
2. clear _____ the beginning
3. he started _____ one end
4. every book _____ it
5. _____ his telegraph office
6. _____ 1876
7. a cot _____ his laboratory
8. station _____ New York
9. died _____ the age _____ 84
10. _____ honor _____ this genius

11. the youngest _____ seven children
12. every experiment _____ the book
13. end _____ a bookshelf
14. _____ an on-coming train
15. did not think _____ himself
16. _____ Menlo Park
17. worked _____ hundreds of projects
18. discoveries _____ electronics
18. _____ October 18

Tell the Story of Thomas Edison

Use the words and phrases below:

in Milan, Ohio
school teacher
too many questions
teach him herself
chemistry book
public library
on-coming train

job
his hearing
laboratory
light bulb
electric power station
electronics
turned out

Test Yourself

Read, write, and look again.

Thomas Edison was born on February 11, 1847, in Milan, Ohio. He was the
_____ of seven children in his family. It was clear from the _____ that
Thomas was _____ about everything. He wanted to _____ the "why" and
"how" of everything. Why does water put out _____? How do birds _____? Why
and how and why?

His _____ teacher had no time or patience for such _____. In fact,
he told Thomas' _____ that there was something _____ with Thomas'
brain. Thomas asked too many questions. He was too _____ to control.

His mother was shocked and _____; she knew he was a smart boy. She
_____ him out of school and decided to _____ him herself. From then on,
Thomas never _____ to school and learned only what he wanted to — and he
_____ to learn everything. For example, a chemistry book his mother   .
_____ him interested him very much. He did every _____ in the
book. The public library was also his _____. He started at one end of the bookshelf and _____ every book on it. Then he began _____.

When he was fourteen, he saved the life of a _____ from an on-coming
_____. The child's father was so grateful that he _____ Thomas a _____ in
his telegraph office. There he learned about sending _____ by wire, and
he even improved the process.

At that time, he began to _____ his hearing, and by the time he was an
adult, he was almost totally _____. This did not _____ him from working or
inventing. He did not consider his _____ a tragedy, and _____ never
discouraged him. Yet, he didn't think of _____ as a genius. He once said,
"_____ is one percent inspiration and ninety-nine percent perspiration."

In 1876, he built a science _____ in Menlo Park, New Jersey.
Work was his _____ love; family and friends came second. He enjoyed working
so much that he had little time to _____. When he was _____, he took
short naps. He even had a cot in his laboratory.

He was celebrtated all over the _____ for his _____. He is probably best known for the electric light _____, the phonograph, and the motion picture _____, but he worked on hundreds of projects. He set up the world's first _____ power station in New York. His discoveries in _____ later led to such things as the radio, x-ray _____, and computers.

He died at the age of eighty-four, on October 18, 1931. That night, the nation turned out its _____ in honor of this _____ who made their _____ so much better. He turned night into day.

Number correct _____/47. Put your score on page 134.

Research and Write

Find more information and write a paragraph about one of these topics: (A) another inventor, (B) an invention, (C) Menlo Park, (D) home schooling.

Which of these inventions has been the most important?

In your journal, write about one of these inventions by Edison, or discuss your personal reaction to Edison's contribution to the culture of our time.

U.S. Post Office 1947

JOHN MUIR

1. Dunbar, Scotland
2. Kentucky
3. Florida
4. Yosemite National Park
5. Alaskan Glacier Fields

John Muir

Discuss

Look at the map and the picture and share what you know about:

conservation

wilderness

America's national park system

John Muir

Read

John Muir was born in Scotland. He loved nature. In America he explored wilderness areas and studied nature. He became a very important conservationist. After a visit to the Yosemite Valley, he worked hard to preserve wilderness areas and he helped to establish the national park system.

Answer

1. Where was John Muir born?
2. What did he explore?
3. What did he become?
4. What did he do after he visited the Yosemite Valley?
5. What did he help establish?

Read

John Muir was born in a small village in Dunbar, Scotland on April 21, 1838. Even as a young boy, he loved the out-of-doors. He loved the trees, the flowers, and the sea. They spoke to him in a special way.

John came from a very strict family. His father was a very serious and demanding man. John and his brother had to work very hard on the family farm. They worked from sunrise to sunset, but they took every opportunity to be out-of-doors.

John's family moved to the United States when he was eleven, and John and his brother loved the wild, open spaces near their new home. At school, he was not a very good student. School did not interest him. He didn't like to be inside; nature was his school and teacher. When he went to college, he didn't like that, either, so he dropped out.

He took different jobs. One day, John had a terrible accident at the shop where he was working. A piece of metal flew in his eye, and he went blind. Slowly, after a month or so, his eyesight came back, but that experience changed his life forever. From them on, he knew what he wanted. He would study nature. That would be his life's work.

He quit his job and began hiking in the wilderness. He hiked a thousand miles, from Kentucky to Florida. In 1868, he hiked in the Yosemite Valley in California. It was an incredible experience. He began to study the rocks, mountains, waterfalls, glaciers, and flowers. He loved it all. He couldn't get enough, but there was a big problem.

Ranchers were destroying the area. There would be nothing left for the future. So, John asked Americans to write to Congress to make Yosemite a national park. And Congress did.

John enjoyed traveling all over the world. Wherever he went — to Alaska, Europe, Asia, or Africa — he studied what he saw. He took careful notes and wrote hundreds of articles and several books.

He made Americans aware of the natural treasures of the land. People began taking trips to the places that he described. President Theodore Roosevelt came, too. He also loved the out-of-doors, and they became friends. The president helped establish America's wild lands as national parks.

John died on December 24, 1914, in his daughter's home after a short illness. He said, "As long as I live, I'll hear waterfalls and birds and winds sing," and he helped others do the same. Today there are fifty-five national parks.

Answer These Questions

Write T for true and F for false.

1. _____ John Muir was not born in the United States.

2. _____ He was an excellent student.

3. _____ He didn't like college.

4. _____ An accident blinded him.

5. _____ His eyesight never came back.

6. _____ He hiked from Kentucky to California.

7. _____ The Yosemite Valley was being destroyed.

8. _____ President Roosevelt made Yosemite a national park.

9. _____ John never met President Roosevelt.

10. _____ John did not have any children.

Now go back to the story and check your answers. Write your score here and on page 134.

Number right _____/10

Write

Now what do you know about:

conservation

wilderness

America's National Park System

John Muir

Timeline Scramble

Finish the timeline.

1838 _____   1. Accident at shop

1849 _____   2. Drops out of college

_____   3. Hikes in Yosemite

_____   4. Muir dies

_____   5. *Travels around the world*

1868 _____   6. Family moves to America

_____   7. Born in Scotland

Travels around the world   8. Hikes 1,000 miles

1914 _____   9. Yosemite becomes national park

New Words

Look at the story again and underline nine words that you are not sure of.
Write them below and ask your classmates or teacher about them or look
them up in your dictionary.

_____   _____   _____

_____   _____   _____

_____   _____   _____

Working with Words

Complete the phrases with the best word.

1. born in a small _____   accident

2. spoke to him in a special _____   illness

3. a very strict _____   problem

4. work on the family _____   spaces

5. serious and demanding _____   parks

6. loved the wild, open _____   village

7. he was not a very good _____   farm

8. near their new _____   notes

9. had a terrible _____   treasures

10. there was a big _____   man

11. he took careful _____   student

12. aware of the national _____   family

13. national _____   way

14. after a short _____   home

Tell the Story of John Muir

Use the words and phrases below:

Dunbar, Scotland	Kentucky to Florida
out-of-doors	Yosemite Valley
strict family	a big problem
moved	Congress
college	traveling
accident	made people aware
life's work	President Roosevelt
quit his job	a short illness
hiking	fifty-five

Test Yourself

Read, write, and look again.

John Muir was born in __ small village in Dunbar, Scotland on April 21, 1838. Even as __ young boy, he loved ____ out-of-doors. He loved ____ trees, _____ flowers, and _____ sea. They spoke to him in ___ special way.

John came from ___ very strict family. ____ father was ___ very serious and demanding man. John and _____ brother had to work very hard on ____ family farm. They worked from sunrise to sunset, but they took every opportunity to be out-of-doors.

John's family moved to the United States when he was eleven, and John and ____ brother loved ____ wild, open spaces near _____ new home. At school, he was not ___ very good student. School did not interest him. He didn't like to be inside; nature was _____ school and teacher. When he went to college, he didn't like that, either, so he dropped out.

He took different jobs. One day, John had ___ terrible accident at ____ shop where he was working. ___ piece of metal flew in ____ eye, and he went blind. Slowly, after ___ month or so, _____ eyesight came back, but that experience changed _____ life forever. From them on, he knew what he wanted. He would study nature. That would be _____ life's work.

He quit _____ job and began hiking in _____ wilderness. He hiked ____ thousand miles, from Kentucky to Florida. In 1868, he hiked in _____ Yosemite Valley in California. It was ____ incredible experience. He began to study _____ rocks, mountains, waterfalls, glaciers, and flowers. He loved it all. He couldn't get enough, but there was ___ big problem.

Ranchers were destroying ____ area. There would be nothing left for _____ future. So, John asked Americans to write to Congress to make Yosemite ___ national park. And Congress did.

John enjoyed traveling all over _____ world. Wherever he went — to Alaska, Europe, Asia, or Africa — he studied what he saw. He took careful notes and wrote hundreds of articles and several books.

He made Americans aware of _____ natural treasures of _____ land. People began taking trips to _____ places that he described. President Theodore Roosevelt came, too. He also loved _____ out-of-doors, and they became friends. The president helped establish America's wild lands as national parks.

John died on December 24, 1914, in _____ daughter's home after ___ short illness. He said, "As long as I live, I'll hear waterfalls and birds and winds sing . . ., " and he helped others do _____ same. Today there are fifty-five national parks.

Number correct _____/47. Put your score on page 134.

Research and Write

RESEARCH AND WRITE
Find more information and write a paragraph about one of these topics: (A) Yosemite, (B) national park system, (C) Theodore Roosevelt.

What Do These Mean to You?

Discuss this stamp or these cartoons. Write about them in your journal.

U.S. Post Office 1964

Eleanor Roosevelt

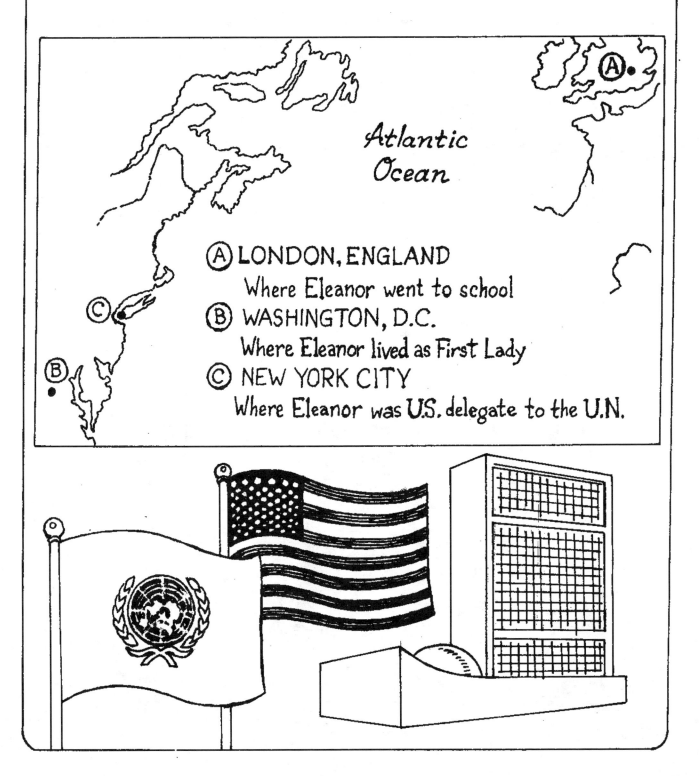

Ⓐ LONDON, ENGLAND
  Where Eleanor went to school
Ⓑ WASHINGTON, D.C.
  Where Eleanor lived as First Lady
Ⓒ NEW YORK CITY
  Where Eleanor was U.S. delegate to the U.N.

Atlantic Ocean

Eleanor Roosevelt

Discuss

Look at the map and the picture and share what you know about:

Eleanor Roosevelt

Franklin D. Roosevelt

The United Nations

The Universal Declaration of Human Rights

Read

Eleanor Roosevelt was the nation's First Lady from 1933 to the death of her husband, President Franklin D. Roosevelt in 1945. These were critical years in American history. The Roosevelts came to Washington during the Great Economic Depression. They guided the country during World War II, and in post-war America, Eleanor was the nation's first delegate to the United Nations.

Answer

1. Who was Eleanor Roosevelt?
2. When was she First Lady?
3. Who was her husband?
4. When did they come to Washington?
5. What did she do in post-war America?

Read

Eleanor Roosevelt was born in 1884 to a well-known family. Her uncle was Theodore Roosevelt, the 26th president of the United States. Life should have been easy for her, but it wasn't. Both of her parents died by the time she was ten years old. She moved into her grandmother's house, but her life wasn't easy there. Her family was not very kind to her. They considered her to be "very plain," even unattractive, because they did not think she was a beautiful woman.

She was sent to school in London, and after her return at the age of 18, she became interested in social issues. She joined the National Consumer League and worked to improve the living conditions of the poor.

In 1905 she married her cousin, Franklin D. Roosevelt. Although the Roosevelts had six children, they did not enjoy a happy relationship. In spite of that, Eleanor supported her husband in his political career. In 1921, Franklin became a victim of polio, and Eleanor often represented him in public because he could only move around in a wheelchair.

Franklin, often called FDR, became president of the United States during the critical years of the Great Economic Depression and World War II. As First Lady, Eleanor continued her work for the poor, for equal rights for all citizens and for civil rights for Black Americans. One of her more dramatic actions was when a famous women's organization cancelled a performance in its hall by Marian Anderson, a great Black singer. Eleanor arranged to have Marian Anderson sing at the Lincoln Memorial. Seventy-five thousand people attended.

With the war finally over, President Truman appointed Eleanor as the U.S. delegate to the United Nations. At the UN, Eleanor worked hard to establish the Universal Declaration of Human Rights. Eleanor was honored when it was published in 1948. After that, Eleanor continued her tireless work for minority rights. Her last official position was the chair of John F. Kennedy's Commission on the Status of Women.

She died in 1962. At her funeral, her friend Adlai Stevenson said, "What other single human being has touched and transformed the existence of so many? She walked in the slums of the world . . . as one who could not feel contentment when others were hungry."

Answer These Questions

Write T for true and F for false.

1. _____ Eleanor's parents died before she was ten years old.

2. _____ Eleanor did not have a happy personal life.

3. _____ Her cousin was Theodore Roosevelt.

4. _____ Her husband was called FDR.

5. _____ When her husband was president, he could not walk.

6. _____ The Roosevelts came to Washington after the Depression.

7. _____ FDR arranged a concert for Marian Anderson.

8. _____ Anderson's concert was a great success.

9. _____ President Kennedy appointed her to the UN.

10. _____ Eleanor helped establish the Universal Declaration of Human Rights.

Now go back to the story and check your answers. Write your score here and on page 134.

Number right _____/10

Write

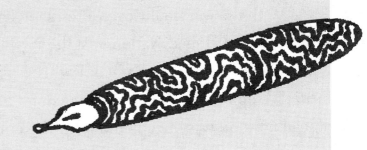

Now what do you know about:

Eleanor Roosevelt
Franklin D. Roosevelt
The United Nations
The Universal Declaration of Human Rights

Timeline Scramble

Finish the timeline.

1884 _____

_____

_____

1905 _____

1933 *Becomes First Lady*

_____

_____

1948 _____

_____

1. FDR gets polio.
2. Serves on the Commission on the Status of Women
3. Delgate to the UN
4. *Becomes First Lady*
5. Marries FDR
6. Declaration of Human Rights
7. Eleanor is born
8. Attends school in London
9. Both parents die
10. Arranges Anderson concert

New Words

Look at the story again and underline nine words that you are not sure of. Write them below and ask your classmates or teacher about them or look them up in your dictionary.

_____ _____ _____

_____ _____ _____

_____ _____ _____

Working with Words

Match these words in column 1 with a word ending in column 2.
Make spelling changes in column 3 if necessary.

1	2	3
1. beauty	a. -ic	1. _beautiful_
2. kind	b. -ance	2. _____
3. consume	c. -less	3. _____
4. relation	d. -ship	4. _____
5. politics	e. -ment	5. _____
6. economy	f. -ity	6. _____
7. depress	g. -ful	7. _____
8. equal	h. -ness	8. _____
9. drama	i. -ion	9. _____
10. perform	j. -er	10. _____
11. tire	k. -tic	11. _____
12. office	l. -ical	12. _____
13. exist	m. -ial	13. _____
14. content	n. -ence	14. _____

Tell the Story of Eleanor Roosevelt

Use these words and phrases:

1884	First Lady
Theodore Roosevelt	Marian Anderson
parents	United Nations
London	Declaration of Human Rights
National Consumer League	Commission on Status of Women
Franklin D. Roosevelt	funeral
polio	slums of the world

Test Yourself

Read, write, and look again.

Eleanor Roosevelt was born in 1884 to a well-known _____. Her _____ was Theodore Roosevelt, the 26th president of the United States. Life should have been easy for her, ____ it wasn't. Both of her _____ died by the time she was ten years old. She moved into her _____ house, _____ her life wasn't easy there. Her _____ was not very kind to her. They considered her to be "very plain," even unattractive, because they did not think Eleanor was a beautiful _____.

She was sent to school in London, and _____ her return at the age of 18, she became interested in _____ issues. She joined the National Consumer League and worked to improve the living conditions of the _____.

In 1905 she married her _____, Franklin D. Roosevelt. _____ the Roosevelts had six _____, they did not enjoy a happy relationship. ___ _____ of that, Eleanor supported her _____ in his political career. In 1921 Franklin became a victim of polio, and Eleanor often represented him in public _____ he could only move around in a wheelchair.

Franklin, often called FDR, became president of the United States _____ the critical years of the Great Economic _____ and World War II. _____ First Lady, Eleanor continued her work for the poor, for equal _____ for all citizens and for civil rights for Black Americans. One of her more dramatic actions was _____ a famous women's organization cancelled a _____ in its hall by Marian Anderson, a great Black _____. Eleanor arranged to have Marian Anderson sing at the Lincoln Memorial. Seventy-five thousand people attended.

_____ the war finally over, President Truman appointed Eleanor as the U.S. delegate to the United Nations. At the UN, Eleanor worked hard to establish the Universal Declaration of _____ Rights. Eleanor was honored _____ it was published in 1948. _____ that, Eleanor continued her tireless work for minority _____. Her last official position was the chair of John F. Kennedy's Commission on the Status of _____.

She died in 1962. At her _____, her friend Adlai Stevenson said, "What other single human _____ has touched and transformed the existence of so many? She walked in the slums of the _____ . . . as one who could not feel contentment when _____ were hungry."

Number correct _____ /36. Put your score on page 134.

Research and Write

Find more information and write a paragraph about one of these topics: (A) Franklin D. Roosevelt, (B) The Great Economic Depression, (C) Marian Anderson, (D) The United Nations, (E) Adlai Stevenson.

What Do These Mean to You?

Discuss these stamps and the personalities of the people shown on them, or write about them in your journal.

U.S. Post Office 1963

U.S. Post Office 1982

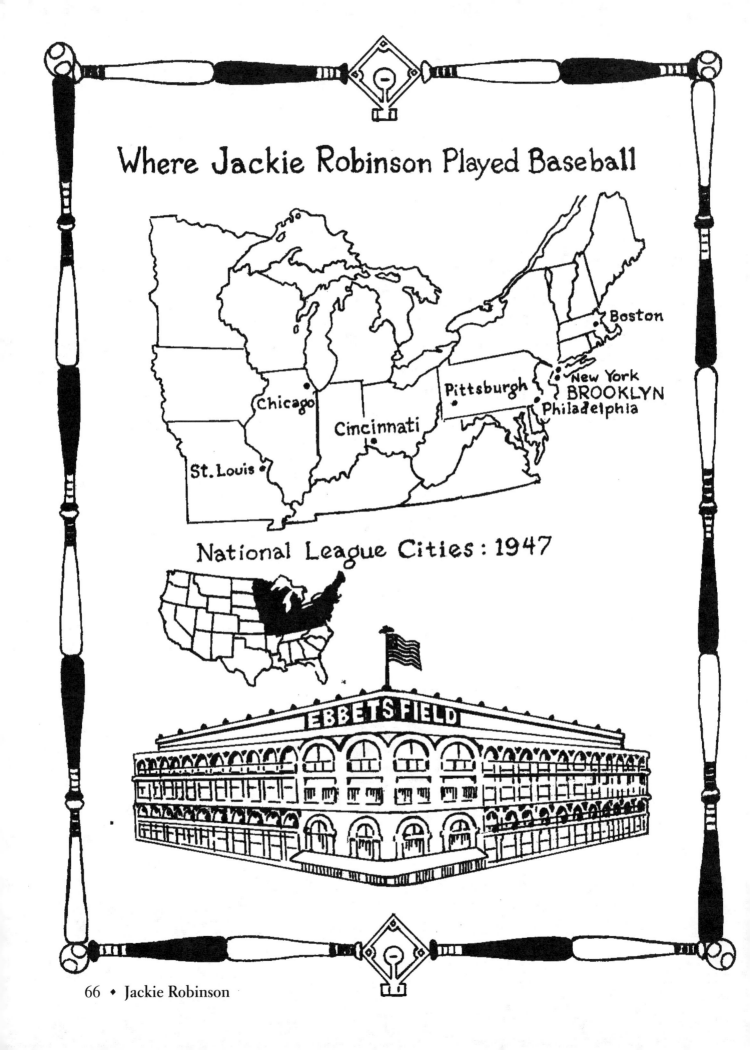

Where Jackie Robinson Played Baseball

National League Cities: 1947

Jackie Robinson

Discuss

Look at the map and the picture and share what you know about:

     racial discrimination

     segregation

     baseball

     Jackie Robinson

Read

In 1945, almost one hundred years after the Emancipation Proclamation, America was still a nation divided by race — Black and White. Discrimination was a fact of life. Everything, especially in the south, was segregated — schools, restaurants, hotels. Baseball was segregated, too. Blacks were not allowed to play with Whites on the same team. Branch Rickey, the general manager of the Brooklyn Dodgers, asked Jackie to join his team. In 1947, Jackie became the first Black player to play on a major all-White team.

Answer

1. What still divided America in 1945?
2. What was segregated?
3. Where was segregation especially strong?
4. Why didn't Blacks and Whites play on the same team?
5. What happened in 1947?

Read

Jackie Robinson was born on January 31, 1919, to a very poor family in Georgia. His family moved to Los Angeles for a better life. There, he went to high school and college, where he played sports. He excelled in all of them — football, basketball, track, and baseball. He was an excellent athlete.

He was a very talented baseball player, but no white professional team would accept him. In 1945, Black players were still excluded from the White professional leagues, called the Major Leagues. Blacks had to play in their own league, the Negro League, which paid much less money.

The owners of the Major League teams didn't want Blacks. They were afraid that fans wouldn't come to the games. Branch Rickey, general manager of the Brooklyn Dodgers, didn't agree. He saw Jackie's talent and wanted him to play. Yet, he knew it wouldn't be easy. The fans, the other teams, and even his own team would make it very difficult for Jackie.

Jackie, however, was ready to fight for his rights. When he was in the army, a bus driver told him all Blacks had to sit in the back of the bus. Jackie refused, and the case was taken to court. Jackie won. Yes, he was a fighter. Now he was ready to fight again.

However, that was exactly what Rickey did not want him to do — fight with anyone, no matter how he was treated. Jackie agreed it would be very difficult.

In 1947, he began to play for the Brooklyn Dodgers. The fans booed, called him terrible names and threw things at him. He even got threats on his life, but he would show them, not with words, but with actions. He played extremely well, and at the end of the year he was named the best new player in his league. In 1949, he was given the Most Valuable Player award. He helped the Dodgers win six National League championships and one World championship.

In 1962, he received baseball's highest award. He was voted into The Baseball Hall of Fame, the first Black, ever. He died on October 24, 1972, a great ball player who had changed the history of sports.

Answer These Questions

Write T for true and F for false.

1. _____ Jackie Robinson was born in Los Angeles.

2. _____ He went to college in Los Angeles.

3. _____ He excelled in several sports.

4. _____ In 1945 Blacks could only play in the National League.

5. _____ Branch Rickey wanted Jackie to play for the Brooklyn Dodgers.

6. _____ Jackie had been in the army.

7. _____ Rickey wanted Jackie to be a fighter.

8. _____ After his first year, Jackie was named the best new player.

9. _____ The Dodgers won six National League championships.

10. _____ He was elected to the Hall of Fame after he died.

Now go back to the story and check your answers. Write your score here and on page 134.

Number right _____/10

Write

Now what do you know about:

racial discrimination

segregation

baseball

Jackie Robinson

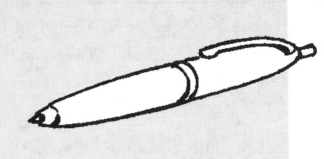

Timeline Scramble

Finish the timeline.

1919	_____	1. Wins Most Valuable Player Award
	_____	2. *Named best new player*
	_____	3. Moves to California
	_____	4. Jackie dies
1947	_____	5. Born in Georgia
.	*Named best new player*	6. Refuses to sit in the back of the bus
1949	_____	7. Begins to play for Brooklyn Dodgers
1962	_____	8. Voted into Hall of Fame
1972	_____	9. Plays sports in college

New Words

Look at the story again and underline nine words that you are not sure of. Write them below and ask your classmates or teacher about them or look them up in your dictionary.

_____ _____ _____

_____ _____ _____

_____ _____ _____

Working with Words

Tell what these people do and did.

Example: player   *plays*   *played*

1. manager   _____   _____
2. owner   _____   _____
3. driver   _____   _____
4. fighter   _____   _____
5. winner   _____   _____
6. visitor   _____   _____
7. explorer   _____   _____
8. interpreter   _____   _____
9. reader   _____   _____
10. publisher   _____   _____
11. traveler   _____   _____
12. speaker   _____   _____
13. rider   _____   _____
14. inventor   _____   _____
15. hiker   _____   _____
16. farmer   _____   _____

Tell the Story of Jackie Robinson

Use these words and phrases:

January 31, 1919	bus driver
Los Angeles	threats
1945	show them with actions
Negro League	best new player
Branch Rickey	Most Valuable Player
fans	Hall of Fame
ready to fight	history of sports

Test Yourself

Read, write, and look again.

Jackie Robinson was born on January 31, 1919 to a _____ poor family in Georgia. His family moved to Los Angeles for a _____ life. There, he went to _____ school and college, where he played sports. He excelled in _____ of them — football, basketball, track, and baseball. He was an _____ athlete.

He was a _____ talented baseball player, but no _____ professional team would accept him. In 1945, _____ players were still excluded from the White _____ leagues, called the Major Leagues. Blacks had to play in their _____ league, the Negro League, which paid _____ less money.

The owners of the Major _____ teams didn't want Blacks. They were _____ that fans wouldn't come to the games. Branch Rickey, _____ manager of the Brooklyn Dodgers, didn't agree. He saw _____ talent and wanted him to play. Yet, he knew it wouldn't be _____. The fans, the _____ teams, and even his _____ team would make it very _____ for Jackie.

Jackie, however, was _____ to fight for his rights. When he was in the army, a bus _____ told him all Blacks had to sit in the _____ of the bus. Jackie refused, and the case was taken to court. Jackie won. Yes, he was a fighter. Now he was _____ to fight again.

However, that was _____ what Rickey did not want him to do — fight with _____, no matter how he was _____. Jackie agreed it would be _____ difficult.

In 1947, he began to play for the Brooklyn Dodgers. The fans booed, called him _____ names and threw things at him. He even got threats on _____ life, but he would show them, not with _____, but with actions. He played _____ well, and at the end of the year he was named the _____ new player in his league. In 1949, he was given the _____ Valuable Player award. He helped the Dodgers win six National _____ championships and one World championship.

In 1962, he received baseball's _____ award. He was voted into The Baseball Hall of Fame, the _____ Black, ever. He died on October 24, 1972, a _____ ball player who had changed the history of _____.

Number correct _____/25. Put your score on page 134.

Research and Write

Find more information and write a paragraph about one of these topics:
(A) baseball, (B) Negro Leagues, (C) Baseball Hall of Fame,
(D) Jackie's life after baseball

Jackie Robinson's plaque in the Baseball Hall of Fame in Cooperstown, New York

"JACK ROOSEVELT ROBINSON, BROOKLYN N.L. 1947-1956. LEADING N.L. BATTER IN 1949. HOLDS FIELDING MARK FOR SECOND BASEMEN PLAYING IN 150 OR MORE GAMES WITH .992. LED N.L. IN STOLEN BASES IN 1947 AND 1949. MOST VALUABLE PLAYER IN 1949. LIFETIME BATTING AVERAGE .311. JOINT RECORD HOLDER FOR MOST DOUBLE PLAYS BY SECOND BASEMEN .137 IN 1951. LED SECOND BASEMEN IN DOUBLE PLAYS IN 1949-50-51-52.

What Does This Mean to You?

Discuss this stamp or write about it in your journal.

U.S. Post Office 1982

Dr. Jonas Salk

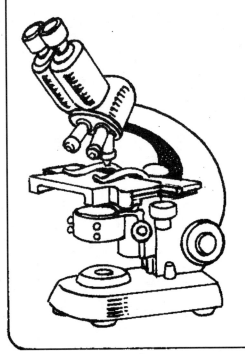

A. New York City
where Salk was born and went to school

B. University of Michigan
where Salk helped develop a flu vaccine

C. University of Pittsburgh
where Salk developed his polio vaccine

D. La Jolla, California
The Salk Institute for Biological Studies

Dr. Jonas Salk

Discuss

Look at the map and the picture and share what you know about:

children's diseases
polio
vaccine
Dr. Jonas Salk

Read

In the 1940s and early 1950s, there was a terrible disease. It was called polio-myelitis or polio. It was a children's disease, and it made many children crippled. Parents everywhere were very worried because no one knew how children got the disease or how to cure it. Doctor Jonas Salk discovered a polio vaccine that saved children. He was a medical hero.

Answer

1. What is the name of the "terrible disease?"
2. Who did the disease affect?
3. What did the disease do to them?
4. Why was everyone afraid of the disease?
5. What did Dr. Jonas Salk do?

Read

Doctor Jonas Salk was born in New York City on October 28, 1914. He was the son of Polish-Jewish immigrants. His parents were not well-educated, but they wanted their son to go to college. They did not have enough money to send him there, so Jonas worked after school and on Saturdays. He was a good student, and he got some scholarships. He enrolled in the College of Medicine of New York University at sixteen and graduated in 1939.

Salk worked at the University of Michigan, where he became very interested in virology, the study of viruses. From 1940 to 1942, he helped to develop an influenza (flu) vaccine. But his most important work came at the University of Pittsburgh. That was where he and a very dedicated staff worked to find a cure for polio.

After eight long years, they announced to the world that they had discovered a vaccine for polio. First, Salk tested the vaccine on himself, his wife, and two sons. It was a brave act, but he knew that it was safe. After that, thousands and thousands of children were vaccinated.

The day the announcement was made was a special day in American history. It was April 12, 1955. People all over the world rejoiced. No more fear of this disease! The disease was conquered. People in cars honked their horns. They rang church bells, and schools were closed. It was a wonderful day.

Doctor Salk became famous. He appeared on televison and radio. Someone suggested that he get a patent for the vaccine and become rich, but he refused. "There is more to life than money," he said.

In 1963, Jonas Salk founded the Salk Institute for Biological Studies in La Jolla, California. He brought together scientists from all over the world to do medical research.

He died on June 23, 1995, at the age of eighty, from heart failure. He will always be remembered as the doctor who saved children.

Answer These Questions

Write T for true and F for false.

1. _____ Jonas Salk's parents were born in New York City.

2. _____ He graduated from the University of Michigan.

3. _____ He helped develop a vaccine for influenza.

4. _____ His most important work was done at the University of Pittsburgh.

5. _____ In a very short time he found a vaccine for polio.

6. _____ Salk tested the vaccine on himself and his family.

7. _____ He never became famous.

8. _____ He got a patent for the vaccine.

9. _____ Salk founded a research institute in California.

10. _____ At eighty, his heart failed.

Now go back to the story and check your answers. Write your score here and on page 134.

Number right _____/10

Write

Now what do you know about:

children's diseases

polio

vaccine

Dr. Jonas Salk

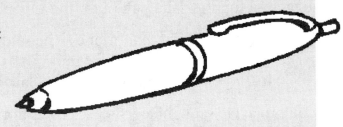

Timeline Scramble

Finish the timeline.

1914	*Dr. Salk born*	1. Works on flu vaccine
	_____	2. Graduates from college
1939	_____	3. Tests vaccine
1940-42	_____	4. Founds Salk Institute
	_____	5. *Dr. Salk born*
1955	_____	6. Polio vaccine announced
1963	_____	7. Dr. Salk dies
1995	_____	8. Enrolls in college

New Words

Look at the story again and underline nine words that you are not sure of. Write them below and ask your classmates or teacher about them or look them up in your dictionary.

_____   _____   _____

_____   _____   _____

_____   _____   _____

Working with Words

Change these "ed" words to nouns. Use *-ion* or *-ment*.

Example: celebrated   *celebration*

1. educated _____
2. enrolled _____
3. graduated _____
4. restored _____
5. developed _____
6. dedicated _____
7. announced _____
8. vaccinated _____
9. suggested _____
10. moved _____
11. founded _____
12. described _____

13. entertained _____
14. collected _____
15. divided _____
16. memorized _____
17. invented _____
18. established _____
19. retired _____
20. added _____
21. recognized _____
22. explored _____
23. excited _____
24. proclaimed _____

Tell the Story of Dr. Jonas Salk

Use these words and phrases:

October 28, 1914
Polish-Jewish
College of Medicine
University of Michigan
influenza
University of Pittsburgh

after eight long years
tested the vaccine
announcement
patent
Salk Institute
June 23, 1995

Test Yourself

Read, write, and look again.

_____ Jonas Salk was born in New York City on October 28, 1914. He was the son of Polish-Jewish _____. His _____ were not well-educated, but they wanted their _____ to go to college. They did not have enough _____ to send him there, so he worked after school and on Saturdays. He was a good _____, and he got some _____. He enrolled in the College of _____ of New York University at sixteen and graduated in 1939.

Salk worked at the _____ of Michigan, where he became very interested in virology, the study of _____. From 1940 to 1942, he helped to develop an influenza (flu) _____. But his most important _____ came at the University of Pittsburgh. That was where he and a very dedicated _____ worked to find a cure for _____.

After eight long _____, they announced to the world that they had discovered a _____ for polio. First, Salk tested the _____ on himself, his wife, and two sons. It was a brave act, but he knew that it was safe. After that, thousands and thousands of _____ were vaccinated.

The day the _____ was made was a special _____ in American history. It was April 12, 1955. _____ all over the world rejoiced. No more fear of that disease! The _____ was conquered. _____ in cars honked their horns. They rang church _____, and schools were closed. It was a wonderful day.

Doctor Salk became famous. He appeared on _____ and radio. Someone suggested that he get a _____ for the vaccine and become rich, but he refused. "There is more to _____ than money," he said.

In 1963, Jonas Salk founded the Salk _____ for Biological Studies in La Jolla, California. He brought together _____ from all over the _____ to do medical _____.

He died on June 23, 1995, at the age of eighty, from heart _____. He will always be remembered as the doctor who saved the _____.

Number correct _____/39. Put your score on page 134.

Research and Write

Find more information and write a paragraph about one of these topics:
(A) polio, (B) influenza, (C) the University of New York,
(D) the University of Michigan, (E) the University of Pittsburgh.

What Does This Mean to You?

Discuss this stamp or write about it in your journal.

U.S. Post Office 1957. Stamp enlarged.

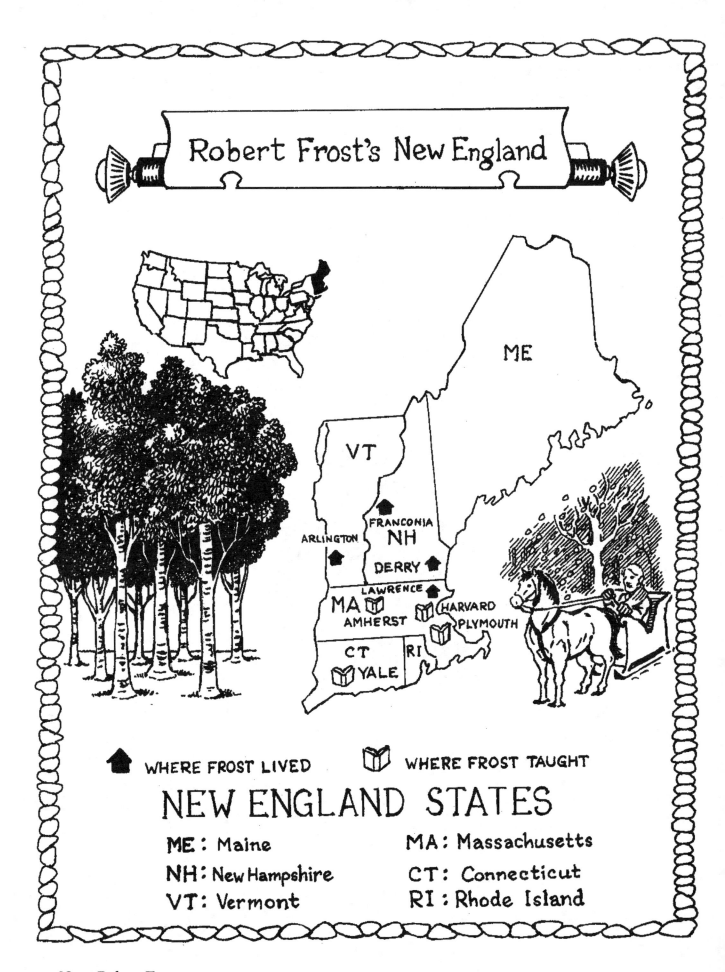

Robert Frost's New England

ME

VT

FRANCONIA
NH

ARLINGTON

DERRY

LAWRENCE

MA
AMHERST   HARVARD
                 PLYMOUTH

CT
YALE   RI

🏠 WHERE FROST LIVED   📖 WHERE FROST TAUGHT

NEW ENGLAND STATES

ME: Maine   MA: Massachusetts
NH: New Hampshire   CT: Connecticut
VT: Vermont   RI: Rhode Island

Robert Frost

Discuss

Look at the map and the picture and share what you know about:

poetry

American poetry

New England

Inauguration Day

Read

Robert Frost is one of America's most important poets. In his poems he wrote about human themes — friendship, love, beauty, sorrow, and death. Many of his poems are set in the landscape of New England. He was also America's first inaugural poet. He spoke at the inauguration of John F. Kennedy in 1961.

Answer

1. Who is Robert Frost?
2. What did he write?
3. Describe his poetry.
4. What did he do at John F. Kennedy's inauguration?

Read

Robert Frost was born in San Francisco, California on March 26, 1874. When he was eleven years old, his father died, and the family moved back to New England. They moved to Massachusetts, where his family had come from. Even as a young boy, Robert loved to write poetry, and he continued to write throughout his life.

He quickly picked up the speech and customs of New Englanders. He also noticed the stark and beautiful New England landscape and wrote about that. He wrote about people and the problems of life. In one of his poems, "Mending Wall," he wrote: "Something there is that doesn't love a wall."

Even though he loved to write poetry, it was difficult to support his family. He was almost always in debt. In addition, two of his children died. Robert was depressed again and again.

He tried many different jobs — teaching, newspaper reporting, and farming, but he still continued to write poetry. Then he moved to England because he thought it would be easier to live there.

Finally, when he was almost forty, he began to be successful as a poet in England. When World War One (WWI) began, he moved back to New England. After that, he won many awards for his poetry.

John F. Kennedy was especially fond of his poetry. In fact, he would often recite his favorite lines from "Stopping by Woods on a Snowy Evening."

> The woods are lovely, dark and deep.
> But I have promises to keep,
> And miles to go before I sleep,
> And miles to go before I sleep.

When Kennedy was elected president, he asked Robert Frost to recite a poem at his inauguration. Frost was deeply honored. It would be the first time a poet would speak at an inauguration. Frost accepted.

Inauguration Day was January 20, 1961. It was cold, and a sharp wind blew as the eighty-seven year old poet began to read. Many wondered whether he would be able to do it; he was no longer a young man, and the weather was against him.

At first, he began quietly. Then his voice became stronger and younger. Finally he recited "The Gift Outright" by heart. When he finished, the crowd cheered and applauded one of America's greatest poets.

Answer These Questions

Write T for true and F for false.

1. ____ Robert Frost was born in New England.

2. ____ When he went to college, he began to write poetry.

3. ____ He wrote about the landscape of England.

4. ____ It was difficult to support his family with poetry.

5. ____ One of his children died.

6. ____ He lived in England for a while.

7. ____ He moved back to America when World War Two (WWII) began.

8. ____ Frost was the first poet to read at an inauguration.

9. ____ Inauguration day is in July.

10. ____ He recited "Mending Wall" at the inauguration.

Now go back to the story and check your answers. Write your score here and on page 134.

Number right _____/10

Write

Now what do you know about: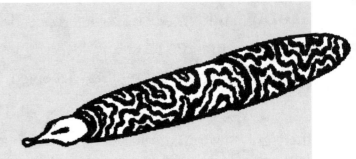

poetry

American poetry

New England

Inauguration Day

Robert Frost

Timeline Scramble

Finish the timeline.

1874	_____
1885	_____
	_____
1914	*World War I begins*
	_____
	_____
	_____
1961	_____
1963	_____

1. Moves back to America
2. Accepts Kennedy's invitation
3. Reads at inauguration
4. Moves to New England
5. Frost dies
6. Kennedy invites Frost to
    read at inauguration
7. Moves to England
8. *World War I begins*
9. Born in San Francisco

New Words

Look at the story again and underline nine words that you are not sure of.
Write them below and ask your classmates or teacher about them or look
them up in your dictionary.

_____   _____   _____

_____   _____   _____

_____   _____   _____

Working with Words

Change the past time to the past progressive time.

Example: He wrote _He was writing_

they moved _____

he continued _____

he supported _____

they ate _____

he taught _____

he reported _____

he farmed _____

he began _____

he won _____

he recited _____

he accepted _____

they began _____

he finished _____

they wondered _____

they cheered _____

they applauded _____

Tell the Story of Robert Frost

Use these words and phrases:

March 26, 1874   England

Massachusetts   World War I

speech and customs   awards

landscape   John F. Kennedy

"Mending Wall"   inauguration

debt   weather

depressed   "The Gift Outright"

Test Yourself

Read, write, and look again.

Robert Frost was born in San Francisco, California on March 26, 1874.
_____ he was eleven years old, his father died, _____ the family moved back to New England. They moved to Massachusetts _____ his family had come from.
_____ as a young boy, Robert loved to write poetry, _____ he continued to write _____ his life.

He _____ picked up the speech _____ customs of New Englanders. He _____ noticed the stark and beautiful New England landscape _____ wrote about that. He wrote about people _____ the problems of life. In one of his poems, "Mending Wall," he wrote:
"Something there is that doesn't love a _____."

_____ though he loved to write poetry, it was difficult to support his family.
He was almost _____ in debt. ___ _____, two of his children died. Robert was depressed _____ and again.
He tried _____ different jobs — teaching, newspaper repoting, and farming, but he _____ continued to write poetry. _____ he moved to England _____ he thought it would be easier to live there.

_____, when he was almost forty, he began to be successful _____ a poet in England. When World War One (WWI) began, he moved back to New England.
_____ that, he won many awards for his poetry.

John F. Kennedy was _____ fond of his poetry. ___ _____, he would often recite his _____ lines from "Stopping by Woods on a Snowy Evening."

The woods are lovely, dark and _____.
_____ I have promises to keep,
And _____ to go before I sleep,
And miles to go before I _____.

_____ Kenndy was elected president, he asked Robert Frost to recite a _____ at his inauguration. Frost was _____ honored. It would be the _____ time a poet _____ speak at an inauguration. Frost accepted.

Inauguration Day was January 20, 1961. It was cold, _____ a sharp wind blew _____ the eighty-seven year old poet began to read. Many wondered _____ he would be able to do it; he was no _____ a young man, _____ the weather was against him.

___ _____, he began quietly. _____ his voice became stronger and younger. _____ he recited "The Gift Outright" by heart. _____ he finished, the crowd cheered _____ applauded one of America's greatest poets.

Number correct _____ **/48.** Put your score on page 134.

Research and Write

Find more information and write a paragraph about one of these topics: (A) New England, (B) John F. Kennedy, (C) Inauguration Day.

What Do These Mean to You?

Here are some titles of Frost poems. See if you can guess what they are about. Then chose one, read it, and write about it in your journal.

Titles of Frost Poems

A Prayer in Spring
Flower-Gathering
Going for Water
After Apple Picking
The Road Not Taken
An Old Man's Winter Night

The Sound of the Trees
Stopping by Woods on a Snowy Evening
On a Tree Fallen Across the Road
Tree at my Window
Fireflies in the Garden
The Figure in the Doorway

Our Hold on the Planet

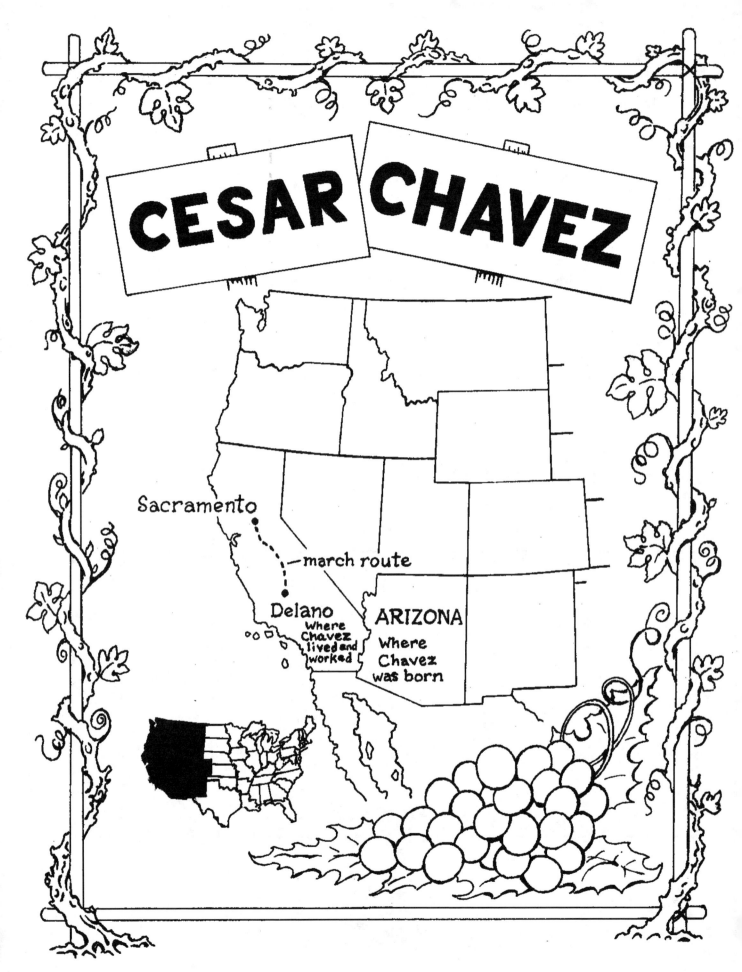

Sacramento

— march route

Delano
Where Chavez lived and worked

ARIZONA
Where Chavez was born

Cesar Chavez

Discuss

Look at the map and the picture and share what you know about:

Migrant farm workers
Labor unions
Boycotts
Non-violence

Read

The year is 1952. In California and in many other states, migrant farm workers work for big companies to pick crops. They travel from farm to farm. Living conditions are terrible. They live in shacks. They work for a few dollars a day. Cesar Chavez is one of these workers. He becomes a labor leader who changes all that.

Answer

1. What do migrant farm workers do?
2. Where do they work?
3. How are their living conditions?
4. How much money do they earn?
5. Who is Cesar Chavez?

Read

Cesar Chavez was a Mexican-American labor leader who was born on March 31, 1927, near Yuma, Arizona. He lived and worked on the family farm until he was eleven years old. Then, in 1939, during the Depression, the family could not pay the taxes on their home and they lost it.

So, the family moved to California to work on the large farms there. They picked lettuce, strawberries, and grapes. They moved from farm to farm. It was back-breaking work. Children often worked, too, even though it was against the law. By the time Cesar graduated from eighth grade, he had attended thirty-eight schools.

Cesar did not like what he saw. Growers often took advantage of the farm workers. Sometimes they cheated them. The workers worked where pesticides were used, and they often got sick. Chavez decided to do something about it.

It wasn't easy, but he organized a union, the National Farm Workers. Would the growers listen to what the workers wanted? The growers were powerful. At first, the growers ignored the union, but slowly Cesar got their attention. He organized strikes, boycotts. and marches. One time, thousands of people marched with him to Sacramento, the capital of California, to protest working conditions. It was a trip of over 200 miles.

He also asked Americans to support the union and the boycott by not buying grapes. Slowly, the nation supported him. They liked his non-violent leadership. He had learned about non-violence as a young man, when he read a book about Gandhi. He liked Gandhi's ideas, and he adopted them. "We can make changes through non-violence," he told his followers.

When strikes and boycotts didn't work, he fasted. Once he didn't eat for twenty-five days. Finally, the growers signed an agreement. The migrant workers got better wages, benefits, and most important, respect.

Cesar Chavez died on April 22, 1993, at the age of sixty-six. Thousands of workers came to his funeral. They wanted to pay respect to this man who had made such a difference in their lives. After he died, he was awarded the Presidential Freedom Award by President Bill Clinton.

Answer These Questions

Write T for true and F for false.

1. _____ Cesar Chavez was born in Mexico.

2. _____ His family could not pay their taxes.

3. _____ He picked fruit and vegetables in California.

4. _____ Children often worked on the farms illegally.

5. _____ Chavez organized the Mexican-American Farm Workers Union.

6. _____ Thousands of workers marched to Los Angeles.

7. _____ Chavez asked Americans to boycott strawberries.

8. _____ Chavez followed the ideas of Gandhi.

9. _____ Once, he fasted for twenty-five days.

10. _____ He was very honored when he received the Presidential Freedom Award.

Now go back to the story and check your answers. Write your score here and on page 134.

Number right _____/10

Write

Now what do you know about:

Migrant farm workers
Labor unions
Boycotts
Non-violence

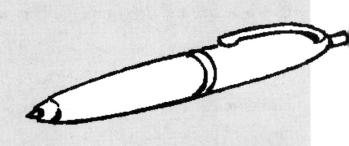

Timeline Scramble

Finish the timeline.

1927	_____
1939	_____
	_____
	_____
	_____
	Growers sign agreement
1993	_____
	_____
	_____

1. Chavez fasts
2. March to Sacramento
3. Receives Freedom Award
4. Organizes a union
5. Chavez dies
6. Family moves to California
7. *Growers sign agreement*
8. Thousands attend funeral
9. Chavez born

New Words

Look at the story again and underline nine words that you are not sure of. Write them below and ask your classmates or teacher about them or look them up in your dictionary.

_____   _____   _____

_____   _____   _____

_____   _____   _____

Working with Words

Change these words into a noun. Use "the."

example: worked   *the work*

lived	_____	lead	_____
pay	_____	believed	_____
move	_____	adopted	_____
graduated	_____	violent	_____
attended	_____	fasted	_____
used	_____	different	_____
organized	_____	agree	_____
decided	_____	important	_____
marched	_____	awarded	_____

Tell the Story of Cesar Chavez

Use these words and phrases:

Mexican-American	strikes
Yuma, Arizona	Sacramento
family farm	boycott
Depression	non-violent
California	Gandhi
farms	fasted
backbreaking	agreement
took advantage of	April 22, 1993
pesticides	funeral
National Farm Workers	Freedom Award

Test Yourself

Read, write, and look again.

Cesar Chavez was a Mexican-American labor leader _____ was born on March 31, 1927, _____ Yuma, Arizona. He lived and worked _____ the family farm _____ he was eleven years old. _____, in 1939, _____ the Depression, the family could not pay the taxes _____ their home and they lost _____.

So, the family moved _____ California to work _____ the large farms there. They picked lettuce, strawberries, and grapes. They moved _____ farm _____ farm. It was backbreaking work. Children _____ worked, too, even _____ it was against the law. _____ the time Cesar graduated _____ eighth grade, he had attended thirty-eight schools. Cesar did not like _____ he saw. Growers _____ took advantage _____ the farm workers. Sometimes they cheated them. The workers worked _____ pesticides were used, and they _____ got sick. Chavez decided to do something _____ it.

It wasn't easy, _____ he organized a union, the National Farm Workers. Would the growers listen to _____ the workers wanted? The growers were powerful. _____ first, the growers ignored the union, _____ slowly Cesar got their attention. He organized strikes, boycotts, and marches. One _____ thousands of people marched _____ him to Sacramento, the capital _____ California, to protest working conditions. It was a trip _____ over 200 miles.

He also asked Americans _____ support the union and the boycott _____ not buying grapes. Slowly, the nation supported him. They liked his non-violent leadership. He had learned about non-violence _____ a young man, _____ he read a book _____ Gandhi. He liked Gandhi's ideas, and he adopted them. "We can make changes _____ non-violence," he told his followers. _____ strikes and boycotts didn't work, he fasted. Once he didn't eat _____ twenty-five days. _____, the growers signed an agreement. The migrant workers got _____ wages, benefits, and _____ important, respect.

Cesar Chavez died ____ April 22, 1993, ____ the age ____ sixty-six. Thousands ____ workers came ____ his funeral. They wanted to pay respect ____ this man ____ had made such a difference ____ their lives. _____ he died, he was awarded the Presidential Freedom Award ____ President Bill Clinton.

Number correct _____ /51. Put your score on page 134.

Research and Write

Find more information and write a paragraph about one of these topics:
(A) The Depression, (B) Labor Unions,
(C) Boycotts, (D) The Presidential Freedom Award.

What Does This Mean to You?

Discuss this map. What do the names of these states have in common? What does this suggest about the history of the United States? Is this important to the present and the future? Write about your ideas and feelings in your journal.

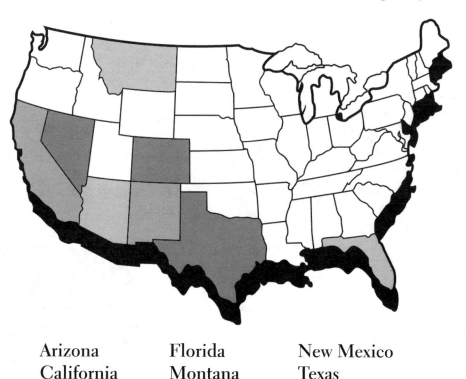

Arizona	Florida	New Mexico
California	Montana	Texas
Colorado	Nevada	

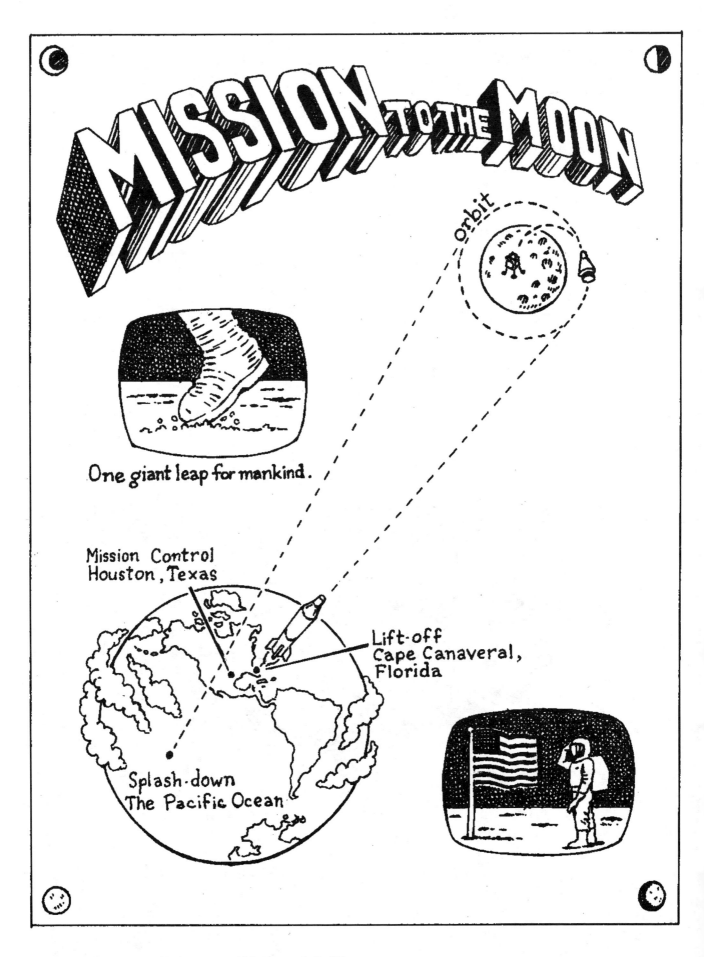

MISSION TO THE MOON

orbit

One giant leap for mankind.

Mission Control
Houston, Texas

Lift-off
Cape Canaveral,
Florida

Splash-down
The Pacific Ocean

Astronauts Armstrong, Aldrin, and Collins

Discuss

Look at the map and the picture and share what you know about:

The moon

Astronauts

NASA

The Eagle

Read

The day is July 20, 1969. Millions of people around the world are watching TV. NASA has launched three astronauts into space to go to the moon, to walk on it, and to come back. The world watches as Neil Armstrong takes the first step on our nearest neighbor in space — the moon.

Answer

1. What has NASA done?
2. What is happening on July 20?
3. How many astronauts have been launched?
4. Who takes the first step on the moon?

Read

When John F. Kennedy became president in 1961, he promised the nation that America would put a man on the moon. Eight years later, that is exactly what happened. The historic launch took place on the morning of July 16, 1969, as NASA launched three astronauts into space.

Neil Armstrong was the commander of this mission. The world watched as he went down the ladder from the Eagle and took the first step onto the moon. Millions watched excitedly and anxiously. They knew that they were seeing one of the most incredible feats of mankind. "That's one small step for a man, one giant leap for mankind," he said.

Neil was followed by Buzz Aldrin. Mike Collins, the third astronaut, piloted the ship while Neil and Buzz explored the moon and gathered rocks to take back to earth.

Landing on the moon had seemed easy and simple. It seemed to go without any problems. But that was not so. Their computer was not working right and did not give good instructions about the landing site; it was a bad place with huge rocks. The landing vehicle, the Eagle, almost crashed. So, Armstrong quickly took manual control of the Eagle and landed it safely in another place. They had only ten seconds of fuel left. It was a close call.

After they landed, they put up the American flag. They also left a plaque on the moon. It read, "Here men from planet Earth first set foot on the moon, July 20, 1969, A.D. We came in peace for all mankind." It was signed by the three astronauts and Richard Nixon, President of the United States.

President Nixon spoke to Neil Armstrong and Buzz Aldrin: "Neil and Buzz . . .

this certainly has to be the most historic telephone call ever made . . . For every American, this has to be the proudest day of our lives . . . And for one priceless moment, in the whole history of man, all people on this earth are truly one."

The men returned safely to earth on July 24. The entire world rejoiced. There were parades everywhere they went — in the United States and other countries. There were official dinners at the White House. They were presented with many awards. America was proud of its astronauts and proud of its great achievement — landing on the moon.

Answer These Questions

Write T for true and F for false.

1. _____ The astronauts went to the moon when Kennedy was president.

2. _____ Armstrong was the commander of the mission.

3. _____ Buzz Aldrin was the second man to step on the moon.

4. _____ Landing on the moon was simple and easy.

5. _____ The Eagle landed on the moon.

6. _____ Collins landed the Eagle safely on the moon.

7. _____ The Eagle had no fuel left when it landed.

8. _____ The astronauts left only the American flag on the moon.

9. _____ President Nixon spoke to the astronauts on a telephone.

10. _____ There were parades in many countries.

Now go back to the story and check your answers. Write your score here and on page 134.

Number right _____/10

Write

Now what do you know about:

The moon
Astronauts
NASA
The Eagle

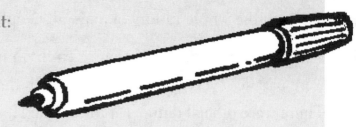

Timeline Scramble

Finish the timeline.

1961	_____	1. Armstrong steps on the moon
July 16, 1969	_____	2. Parades everywhere
July 20	_____	3. Eagle almost crashes
	_____	4. Astronauts return
	_____	5. Kennedy becomes president
	_____	6. *Nixon speaks to astronauts*
	Nixon speaks to astronauts	7. Astronauts put up flag
July 24	_____	8. Aldrin steps on the moon
	_____	9. Astronauts launched

New Words

Look at the story again and underline nine words that you are not sure of.
Write them below and ask your classmates or teacher about them or look
them up in your dictionary.

_____   _____   _____

_____   _____   _____

_____   _____   _____

Working with Words

Change these words to "-ly" adverbs.

Example: exact   _exactly_

excited   _____   slow   _____

anxious   _____   successful   _____

incredible   _____   quiet   _____

easy   _____   brave   _____

simple   _____   special   _____

quick   _____   terrible   _____

safe   _____   extreme   _____

certain   _____   strict   _____

proud   _____   serious   _____

true   _____   curious   _____

official   _____   immediate   _____

Tell the Story of the astronauts.

Use these words and phrases:

John F. Kennedy   Mike Collins

July 16, 1969   landing

NASA   huge rocks

Neil Armstrong   American flag

the Eagle   plaque

the first step   President Nixon

giant leap   July 24

Buzz Aldrin   parades

Test Yourself

Read, write, and look again.

When John F. Kennedy became _____ in 1961, _____ promised the _____ that America would put a _____ on the moon. Eight years later, _____ is exactly what happened. The historic _____ took place on the morning of July 16, 1969, as NASA launched three astronauts into _____.

Neil Armstrong was the _____ of this mission. The _____ watched as ____ went down the ladder from the Eagle and took the first _____ onto the moon. _____ watched excitedly and anxiously. _____ knew that they were seeing _____ of the most incredible feats of _____. "That's one small step for a _____, one giant leap for _____," he said.

Neil was followed by Buzz Aldrin. Mike Collins, the third _____, piloted the ship while Neil and Buzz explored the moon and gathered rocks to take back to _____.

_____ on the moon had seemed easy and simple. It seemed to go without any problems. But _____ was not so. Their computer was not working right and did not give good instructions about the landing site; it was a bad _____ with huge rocks. The landing vehicle, the _____, almost crashed. So, _____ quickly took manual control of the Eagle and landed ____ safely in another _____. They had only ten seconds of fuel left. It was a close call.

After _____ landed, they put up the American flag. _____ also left a plaque on the moon. It read, "Here _____ from planet Earth first set foot on the moon, July 20, 1969, A.D. _____ came in peace for all _____." It was signed by the three astronauts and Richard Nixon, President of the United States.

President Nixon spoke to Neil Armstrong and Buzz Aldrin: "Neil and Buzz . . . _____ certainly has to be the most historic _____ call ever made . . . For every American, _____ has to be the proudest day of _____ lives . . . And for one priceless moment, in the whole history of _____, all _____ on this earth are truly one."

The _____ returned safely to earth on July 24. The entire _____ rejoiced. There were parades everywhere _____ went — in the United States and other _____. There were official dinners at the White House. _____ were presented with many awards. America was proud of _____ astronauts and proud of _____ great achievement — _____ on the moon.

Number correct _____ /45. Put your score on page 134.

Research and Write

Find more information and write a paragraph about one of these topics: A) the moon, (B) NASA, (C) the Eagle, (D) one of the astronauts.

What Does This Mean to You?

Discuss this stamp or write about it in your journal.

U.S. Post Office 1994

Jaime Escalante's Journey

Los Angeles... where Escalante taught.

Puerto Rico... where Escalante went to school.

TEXT

Bolivia... where Escalante was born.

Jaime Escalante

Discuss

Look at the map and the picture and share what you know about:

Inner city schools and gangs

High School dropouts

Calculus

Placement Tests

Read

Jaime Escalante came to America with no money and no English. He learned English, got his teaching degree, and began teaching in one of Los Angeles' worst schools. He believed that all students, rich or poor, could learn. He inspired his students, taught them and expected excellence. His students went from being poor students to being the best in the nation.

Answer

1. What did Escalante have when he came to America?
2. Where did he teach?
3. What did he believe?
4. How did his students do?

Read

Jaime Escalante was born in La Paz, Bolivia in 1930. He got his education in Bolivia and Puerto Rico. He then emigrated to the United States. He came to America with no money and no English, but he knew what hard work was. He worked as a busboy during the day and went to college at night to learn English and get his teaching certificate.

When Escalante began teaching at Garfield High School, an inner city school in Los Angeles, it was one of the worst and poorest schools in the city. The students weren't interested in school, and they weren't interested in learning. The school had a 55% dropout rate. Few students finished high school.

Escalante wanted to change all that. He challenged the students. Did they want to be busboys and dishwashers all their lives? Did they want nothing better? Did they want to be poor all their lives?

He promised them that they could get excellent jobs as engineers, computer specialists and electronics experts, but not without an education and not without math. They would have to work hard, but they could learn, and he would help them.

Escalante began by using non-traditional ways of teaching. He opened every class with a cheer or a saying to inspire the students. He said passion, desire and guts (or in Spanish, "ganas") equal success. "That's all you need," he told them again and again, and they began to believe him.

He began a calculus class. The school administration protested. These students weren't capable of higher mathematics, they said. Escalante proved them wrong. Within three years, his students got top scores on the national Advanced Placement Test.

The officials from the Educational Testing Service didn't believe the scores. It was impossible, they said. The students must have cheated. They took the test again. Again, they got top scores.

In 1987, a movie was made about Jaime Escalante. It was *Stand and Deliver*, and people loved the film and its message. It showed how an inspired teacher changed the lives of students who were involved in gangs and violence, and who had no goals in life.

Presidents Reagan and Bush noted Escalante's success and invited him to the White House. He had become a national hero, and his students were heroes, too.

Answer These Questions

Write T for true and F for false.

1. _____ Jaime Esclante was born in Puerto Rico.

2. _____ He learned English in Puerto Rico.

3. _____ He worked at night in America.

4. _____ He began teaching at a high school.

5. _____ More than half of the students dropped out.

6. _____ He began his classes with a song.

7. _____ He taught calculus.

8. _____ After two years, his students got top scores.

9. _____ His students were tested twice.

10. _____ *Stand and Deliver* is a movie.

Now go back to the story and check your answers. Write your score here and on page 134.

Number right _____/10

Write

Now what do you know about:

Inner city schools and gangs

High school dropouts

Placement tests

Jaime Escalante

Timeline Scramble

Finish the timeline.

1930	*born in Bolivia*	1. Began teaching
		2. *Stand and Deliver* produced
		3. Students re-tested
		4. Educated in Puerto Rico
		5. Began teaching calculus
		6. *Born in Bolivia*
		7. Came to America
1987		8. Students get top scores
		9. Invited to White House

New Words

Look at the story again and underline nine words that you are not sure of. Write them below and ask your classmates or teacher about them or look them up in your dictionary.

_____   _____   _____

_____   _____   _____

_____   _____   _____

Working with Words

Change these verb phrases to questions.

Example: he got *did he get?*

1. he knew   _____
2. he came   _____
3. he worked   _____
4. he went   _____
5. he began   _____
6. it was   _____
7. they finished   _____
8. he wanted   _____
9. they could learn   _____
10. he would help   _____
11. he opened   _____
12. he said   _____

13. he told   _____
14. they protested   _____
15. he proved   _____
16. they cheated   _____
17. they took   _____
18. they admired   _____
19. it showed   _____
20. he changed   _____
21. they had   _____
22. they invited   _____
23. they were   _____

Tell the Story of Jaime Escalante

Use these words and phrases:

La Paz Bolivia	cheer
educated	calculus
emigrated	administration
college	Advanced Placement Test
teaching certificate	Educational Testing Service
Garfield High School	movie
challenged	White House

Test Yourself

Jaime Escalante was born in La Paz, Bolivia in 1930. He _____ his education in Bolivia and Puerto Rico. He then _____ to the United States. He _____ to America with no money and no English, but he _____ what hard work was. He _____ as a busboy during the day and _____ to college at night to learn English and _____ his teaching certificate.

When Escalante _____ teaching at Garfield High School, an inner city school in Los Angeles, it _____ one of the worst and poorest schools in the city. The students _____ interested in school, and they _____ interested in learning. The school _____ a 55% dropout rate. Few students _____ high school.

Escalante _____ to change all that. He _____ the students. Did they _____ to be busboys and dishwashers all their lives? Did they want nothing better? _____ they _____ to be poor all their lives?

He _____ them that they could _____ excellent jobs as engineers, computer specialists and electronics experts, but not without an education and not without math. They _____ have to work hard, but they _____ learn, and he would _____ them.

Escalante _____ by using non-traditional ways of teaching. He _____ every class with a cheer or a saying to inspire the students. He _____ passion, desire and guts (or in Spanish, "ganas") equal success. "That's all you need," he _____ them again and again, and they began to _____ him.

He _____ a calculus class. The school administration _____. These students _____ capable of higher mathematics, they _____. Escalante _____ them wrong. Within three years, his students _____ top scores on the national Advanced Placement Test.

The officials from the Educational Testing Service _____ believe the scores. It _____ impossible, they said. The students must have _____. They _____ the test again. Again, they _____ top scores.

In 1987, a movie was _____ about Jaime Escalante. It was *Stand and Deliver*, and people _____ the film and its message. It _____ how an inspired teacher _____ the lives of students who were _____ in gangs and violence, and who _____ no goals in life.

Presidents Reagan and Bush _____ Escalante's success and _____ him to the White House. He had _____ a national hero, and his students were heroes, too.

Number correct _____ **/49.** Put your score on page 134.

Research and Write

Find more information and write a paragraph about one of these topics:
(A) Bolivia, (B) calculus,
(C) Advanced Placement Test,
(D) a review of *Stand and Deliver*.

What Does This Mean to You?

Watch the video *Stand and Deliver* and then discuss your feeling about it or write about it in your journal.

This is the cover of the video **Stand and Deliver**, "a true story about a modern miracle," starring Edward James Olmos and Lou Diamond Phillips, written by Tom Musca, the producer, and Ramon Menendez, the director. Copyright © 1988 Warner Brothers. Available in video stores.

ADULT DRAMA

He knows his kids are winners. Now they've got to prove it.

Do you like movies that are "funny, suspenseful, inspiring and true?"[1] "Terrific. Tremendously gripping and compelling?"[2] "Sure to make your eyes fill with tears, your heart with hope?"[3] Then you'll love *Stand and Deliver*, the dynamic saga of real-life heroes determined to conquer a foe few people dare confront: the National Advanced Placement Calculus Exam.

Edward James Olmos (*Miami Vice*) gives a fierce, widely-acclaimed performance as Jaime Escalante, a math teacher at East Los Angeles' Garfield High who refuses to write off his inner-city students as losers. Escalante cajoles, pushes, wheedles, needles, threatens and inspires 18 kids who were struggling with fractions and long division to become math whizzes. But are any of them *really* ready for the AP calculus exam...and a ticket out of the barrio? The film's exhilarating ending is even more astonishing because it's true.

A superb cast joins Olmos, including Lou Diamond Phillips (*La Bamba, Young Guns*) as a troublemaker with a secret desire to learn, Andy Garcia (*The Untouchables*) as a suspicious representative of the Educational Testing Service and a bunch of talented, fresh-faced newcomers as the calculus students.

Get ready for "the *Rocky* of the classroom."[4] When Escalante's kids *Stand and Deliver*, you'll stand up and cheer!

1) Charles Champlin, *Los Angeles Times* 2) Jack Kroll, *Newsweek*
3) Joel Siegel, *Good Morning America*/ABC-TV 4) Pat Collins, WWOR-TV

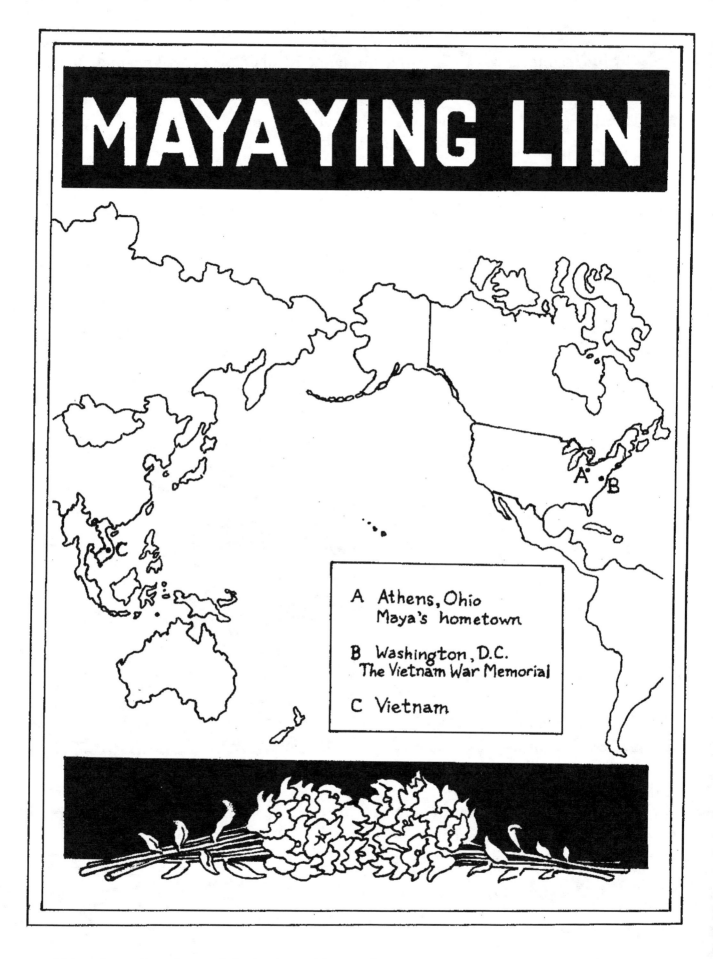

MAYA YING LIN

A Athens, Ohio
   Maya's hometown

B Washington, D.C.
   The Vietnam War Memorial

C Vietnam

Maya Ying Lin
and the Vietnam Memorial

Discuss

Look at the map and the picture and share what you know about:

> Vietnam
> The Vietnam War
> The Vietnam Memorial
> Memorials in Washington, D.C.

Read

The Vietnam War Memorial is a famous monument in Washington, D.C. It honors the veterans of the Vietnam War. Maya Ying Lin was a college student, only twenty-one years old when she entered and won a national contest to design this memorial. Originally, there was much controversy about it, but today it is one of the most admired memorials in America.

Answer

1. Where is the Vietnam War memorial?
2. Who does it honor?
3. What was Maya Lin?
4. How old was she when she entered the contest?

Read

The late 1960s and early 1970s were a terrible time in America's history. There was no end in sight to the Vietnam War. People were tired of war. They didn't want to send their sons to war halfway around the world. Yet, the government kept sending more and more soldiers to Vietnam. Young people, especially, protested. Many refused to go into the military. There were many marches and protests. The war divided the nation.

Finally, on April 30, 1975, the war ended. North Vietnam invaded South Vietnam, and America lost the war. Soldiers who came back from the war were not honored as heroes. Americans everywhere just wanted to forget. It was too painful.

However, the veterans believed they deserved the thanks and respect of the nation. So, in 1979 they set up a committee called the Vietnam Veterans Memorial Fund. But where would they get the money? Many famous people helped them, and soon they had raised over a million dollars.

But what about the design of the memorial? In 1980, a contest was held to design the memorial. Maya Ying Lin was a student at Yale University. She was twenty-one years old, born on October 5, 1959, to Chinese-American parents in Athens, Ohio. Her parents were professors at Ohio University. They had escaped from China in the late 1940s.

She decided to enter the contest, and so she visited Washington, D.C. She wanted to look at the site where the memorial was to be built. It was a beautiful site — peaceful, a little hilly, and surrounded by trees. It looked at the Washington Monument and the Lincoln Memorial. The memorial would look to the past as well as the future, she decided.

She thought a lot about the design. She wanted it to be part of the environment, but the names of the dead veterans should be the central focus of the memorial. She concluded that the names would be the memorial. Each name, she decided would be carved into a wall of black granite. She entered the contest, and to her great surprise, she won.

Almost immediately there was controversy. She was too young. What did she know about war? The design was too simple, and — she was an Asian. But when the design was shown, it received praise from almost everyone, and it was approved.

Finally, on November 13, 1982, Veterans Day, the memorial was opened. People came from everywhere. At the ceremony, each of the 58,193 names was read aloud. It was a powerful experience.

Answer These Questions

Write T for true and F for false.

1. _____ Americans didn't like the Vietnam War.

2. _____ South Vietnam won the war.

3. _____ American soldiers were welcomed home as heroes.

4. _____ Maya Lin was a student when she entered the contest.

5. _____ Her parents were Asians.

6. _____ The site for the memorial was outside Washington.

7. _____ She decided to have the names of all the veterans on the wall.

8._____ Almost immediately there was controversy about the design.

9. _____ The memorial was opened on Veterans Day.

10. _____ More than 58,000 soldiers died in Vietnam.

Now go back to the story and check your answers. Write your score here and on page 134.

Number right _____/10

Write

Now what do you know about:

Vietnam

The Vietnam War

The Vietnam Memorial

Memorials in Washington, D.C.

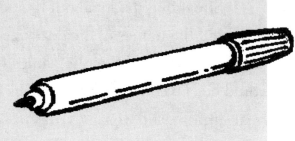

Timeline Scramble

Finish the timeline.

1940s	_____	1. Creates design
1959	_____	2. Enters contest
	Decides to enter contest	3. Design approved
	_____	4. Maya visits D.C.
	_____	5. Memorial is opened
	_____	6. Wins contest
	_____	7. Parents come to America
	_____	8. Maya Lin born
	_____	9. Controversy over design
1982	_____	10. *Decides to enter contest*

New Words

Look at the story again and underline nine words that you are not sure of.
Write them below and ask your classmates or teacher about them or look
them up in your dictionary.

_____   _____   _____

_____   _____   _____

_____   _____   _____

Working with Words

Change these phrases to passive voice:

Examples: They did it   *It was done*

             They saw them   *They were seen*

1. They sent them   _____

2. They protested the war   _____

3. It divided the nation   _____

4. They invaded the south   _____

5. It lost the war   _____

6. They raised the money   _____

7. They held a contest   _____

8. They showed the design   _____

9. They approved it   _____

10. They opened the memorial   _____

11. They read the names   _____

Tell the Story of Maya Ying Lin

Use these words and phrases:

late 1960s; early 1970s	Ohio University
government	Washington, D.C.
marches and protests	design
April 30, 1975	black granite
North Vietnam	controversy
committee	Asian
contest	November 13, 1982

Test Yourself

Read, write, and look again.

The late 1960s and early 1970s were a terrible _____ in America's history. There was no end in sight to the _____ War. People were tired of _____. They didn't want to send their _____ to war halfway around the _____. Yet, the government kept sending more and more _____ to Vietnam. Young people especially, protested. Many refused to go into the _____. There were many marches and _____. The war divided the _____.

Finally, on April 30, 1975, the war ended. North Vietnam invaded _____ Vietnam, and America lost the war. Soldiers who came back from the _____ were not honored as _____. Americans everywhere just wanted to forget. It was too painful.

However, the _____ believed they deserved the _____ and _____ of the nation. So, in 1979 they set up a _____ called the Vietnam Veterans Memorial Fund. But where would they get the _____? Many famous _____ helped them and soon they had raised over a million _____.

But what about the design of the _____? In 1980, a contest was held to design the memorial. Maya Ying Lin was a _____ at Yale University. She was twenty-one years old, born on October 5, 1959, to Chinese-American _____ in Athens, Ohio. Her parents were professors at Ohio University. They had escaped from _____ in the late 1940s.

She decided to enter the _____, and so she visited Washington, D.C. She wanted to look at the _____ where the memorial was to be built. It was a beautiful site — peaceful, a little hilly, and surrounded by _____. It looked at the Washington Monument and the Lincoln Memorial. The memorial would look to the _____ as well as the future, she decided.

She thought a lot about the _____. She wanted it to be part of the _____, but the names of the dead _____ should be the central focus of the memorial. She concluded that the _____ would be the memorial.

Each name, she decided would be carved into a _____ of black granite. She entered the contest, and to her great _____, she won.

Almost immediately there was _____. She was too young. What did she know about war? The design was too simple, and — she was an _____. But when the design was shown, it received _____ from almost everyone, and it was approved.

Finally, on November 13, 1982, Veterans Day, the memorial was opened. People came from _____. At the ceremony, each of the 58,193 names was read aloud. It was a powerful _____.

Number correct _____/38. Put your score on page 134.

Research and Write

Find more information and write a paragraph about one of these topics:
(A) Vietnam, (B) the Vietnam War,
(C) the Washington Monument, (D) the Lincoln Memorial.

What Does This Mean to You?

Discuss this stamp or write about it in your journal.

U.S. Post Office 1984. This stamp has been blown up.

The ORDINARY CITIZEN

The Ordiary Citizen

Discuss

Share what you have learned so far about American history.

Read

There have been many heroes throughout American history, but the most important hero is the Ordinary Citizen, doing ordinary and extraordinary things day after day.

In December of 1620, 103 immigrants from England, known as the Pilgrims, arrived in Plymouth, Massachusetts, after three months aboard their small ship, the Mayflower. During the first winter, half of them died. However, with the help of the Native Americans, many survived to celebrate their first year in their new land in November, 1621. Together with the Native Americans they held a feast of Thanksgiving, now an important holiday.

Before and after the Declaration of Independence on July 4, 1776, many explorers traveled throughout the North American continent. Lewis and Clark, with Sacagawea, are well-known explorers of the American West, but they didn't go alone, and they weren't the only or the first explorers of the continent. Many hundreds of Europeans explored the unknown West, slowly making the unknown, known.

As more and more immigrants arrived, they moved westward to find new homes for themselves. Called pioneers, they gradually, slowly, and often painfully crossed the continent in wagons. Along the way many died, and many stopped and settled down, developing the rich heart of the continent.

Unfortunately, the westward movement resulted in a terrible confict with the Native American nations. This struggle brought great suffering to the pioneers and even more suffering to the Native Americans as they tried to defend their land and their way of life. There were heroic deeds on both sides, but the ultimate effect of these terrible times lives on in contemporary America where many Native Americans still live difficult lives on reservations.

In 1869, the continent was finally opened to railroad travel from coast to coast. Thousands of immigrants, especially Irish and Chinese, worked long and hard to build the transcontinental railway. As America's industry grew in the 19th century, so did its cities, and in 1883, workers in Chicago began to work on the first skyscraper — ten stories high. You can find the architect's name in a history book, but the dangerous work was done by ordinary Americans, many of them Native Americans and immigrants.

In the 18th and 19th centuries, the practice of slavery brought millions of Africans to America, especially to the southern states. These African Americans lived and suffered under terrible conditions. Many struggled for their freedom and their rights. Some bravely escaped to the North for a better life. Even after slavery ended with the Civil War, most African-Americans did not have happy lives. Finally, by the middle of the 20th century, many courageous thousands joined the non-violent civil rights movement under the leadership of Martin Luther King, Jr., to demand equal rights and opportunity. Although racial prejudice still exists today, the determination of countless and nameless African-Americans is beginning to result in a society that Lincoln could only dream of.

America has seen many wars, and although the leaders of these wars are famous, once again, ordinary Americans carried out the battles. Everybody knows George Washington, but few people know the names of the "embattled farmers" who faced the British army at the Battle of Lexington and Concord and fired "the shot heard round the world."

In the mid-nineteenth century, the evil of slavery helped to cause the American Civil War. Thousands on both sides bravely volunteered to fight for their cause. 215,000 of them died on the battlefield, and many more soldiers and civilians lost their lives before it was over.

In the 20th century, America could no longer stay out of the politics and wars of the "Old World." In World War I, American "Doughboys" went to France, and American women followed along as nurses. Soldiers on all sides faced great horrors as tanks, airplanes and poison gas were used for the first time.

After the War, ordinary Americans faced another challenge — the great economic depression of the 1930s. Banks failed, the stock market crashed, industrial production fell, farmers lost their farms, and, at times, unemployment was over 25%.

These were difficult times, and some lost hope, but slowly and surely people found the courage to regain their losses and go back to work.

On December 7, 1941, America was again at war in World War II. Millions of citizens became soldiers, and the citizen soldiers, now known as "G.I. Joe," proved once again that ordinary Americans from the big cities to the small towns could serve their country well. At the same time, American women, symbolized by "Rosie the Riveter," went to work in American industries to replace the men and help win the war.

Then came the Cold War. Americans helped save the small country of South Korea from Communist aggression. In the sixties and seventies, America tried to do the same thing in Viet Nam. It was a terrible time in American history. Thousands were asked to serve their country again. Many did so, and many died in a war that nobody wanted. At the same time, thousands more protested the war and eventually forced the government to abandon South Viet Nam.

Now, a new page in American history has begun with the terrorist attacks on the World Trade Center and the Pentagon on September 11, 2001. In the air over Pennsylvania, a handful of passengers forced their hijacked plane to crash before it could reach Washington, D.C. And in New York City at the World Trade Center, 350 firefighters and police officers died as they tried to save others. For years, the firefighters and the police had been the unsung heroes of the land, but sadly it took an act of terrorism to give these public servants the respect and honor they have always deserved.

Famous heroes come and go, and live on in history, but the ordinary heroes will always be there, unsung and nameless.

Tell the Story of the Ordinary Citizen

Use the information below.

December, 1620, Pilgrims

November 1621

July 4, 1776

explorers

pioneers

Native Americans

slavery

Civil War

1869, transcontinental railway

World War I

the Great Depression

World War II

the Cold War

the civil rights movement

Viet Nam

September 11, 2001

Review

Use the information in this book to construct a timeline from the 16th century through the 20th century.

Talk

Pretend you are one of the heroes in this book. Introduce yourself to the class, and talk about your life, or have a classmate interview you.

Discuss

Tell each other which hero is your favorite. Explain why.

Write and Perform

You can perform a play about a hero from the book, *Celebrating American Heroes*. Three of the heroes are not in the play book. Write and perform a play about Eleanor Roosevelt, Maya Lin, or An Ordinary Citizen.

Research

There are many heroes in American history. This book tells about only a few. Choose another hero and write or tell about them.

Here are some suggestions:

Benjamin Franklin	Booker T. Washington
Thomas Jefferson	Amelia Earhart
Walt Whitman	Dwight Eisenhower
Mark Twain	John F. Kennedy
Muhammad Ali	Rachel Carson
Martin Luther King, Jr.	Helen Keller
Frederick Douglass	Chief Joseph of the Nez Percé
Marian Anderson	Robert E. Lee

Discuss or Write

History continues, from day to day. What has happened since this book was written? What will happen in your lifetime?

Answers for
Working with Words *Exercises*

Betsy Ross, George Washington, and the American Flag

1. lives
2. families
3. churches
4. shops
5. flags
6. colonies
7. countries
8. historians
9. speeches
10. stories

Sacagawea

1. important (part)
2. terrible (times)
3. valuable (addition)
4. strong (horses)
5. easy (crossing)
6. long and dangerous (journey)
7. (often) hungry
8. courageous (woman)
9. young (son)
10. fine (gentleman)

Dolley Madison

1. move
2. marry
3. entertain
4. invade
5. refuse
6. restore
7. cover
8. retire
9. insist
10. enter

Harriet Beecher Stowe

1. married
2. appeared
3. wanted
4. happened
5. ignited
6. treated
7. divided
8. visited
9. started
10. signed
11. remembered
12. chanted
13. cheered
14. smiled
15. bowed
16. died

Abraham Lincoln and the Gettysburg Address

1. they thought
2. they invited
3. they loved
4. he accepted
5. he knew
6. they wanted
7. they cared
8. he put
9. the day came
10. thousands came
11. he rode
12. they realized
13. he thought
14. he told
15. they memorized

Thomas Alva Edison

1. on February 11
2. of seven children
3. from the beginning
4. in the book
5. at one end
6. of the bookshelf
7. on it
8. from an on-coming train
9. in his telegraph office
10. of himself
11. in 1876
12. in Menlo Park
13. in his laboratory
14. on hundreds
15. in New York
16. in electronics
17. at the age of 84
18. on October 18
19. in honor of this genius

John Muir

1. a small village
2. in a special way
3. strict family
4. the family farm
5. demanding man
6. open spaces
7. good student
8. new home
9. terrible accident
10. a big problem
11. careful notes
12. national treasures
13. national parks
14. short illness

Eleanor Roosevelt

1. beauti*ful*
2. kind*ness*
3. consum*er*
4. relation*ship*
5. polit*ical*
6. econom*ic*
7. depress*ion*
8. equal*ity*
9. drama*tic*
10. perform*ance*
11. tire*less*
12. offic*ial*
13. exist*ence*
14. content*ment*

Jackie Robinson

1. manages — managed
2. owns — owned
3. drives — drove
4. fights — fought
5. wins — won
6. visits — visited
7. explores — explored
8. interprets — interpreted
9. reads — read
10. publishes — published
11. travels — traveled
12. speaks — spoke
13. rides — rode
14. invents — invented
15. hikes — hiked
16. farms — farmed

Jonas Salk

1. education
2. enrollment
3. graduation
4. restoration
5. development
6. dedication
7. announcement
8. vaccination
9. suggestion
10. movement
11. foundation
12. description
13. entertainment
14. collection
15. division
16. memorization
17. invention
18. establishment
19. retirement
20. addition
21. recognition
22. exploration
23. excitement
24. proclamation

Robert Frost

1. they were moving
2. he was continuing
3. he was supporting
4. they were eating
5. he was teaching
6. he was reporting
7. he was farming
8. he was beginning
9. he was winning
10. he was reciting
11. he was accepting
12. they were beginning
13. he was finishing
14. they were wondering
15. they were cheering
16. they were applauding

Cesar Chavez

1. the life
2. the pay, payment
3. the move, movement
4. the graduation, graduate
5. the attendance
6. the use
7. the organization
8. the decision
9. the march
10. the leadership, leader
11. the belief
12. the adoption
13. the violence
14. the fast
15. the difference
16. the agreement
17. the importance
18. the award

Astronauts Armstrong, Aldrin, and Collins

1. excitedly
2. anxiously
3. incredibly
4. easily
5. simply
6. quickly
7. safely
8. certainly
9. proudly
10. truly
11. officially
12. slowly
13. successfully
14. quietly
15. bravely
16. specially
17. terribly
18. extremely
19. strictly
20. seriously
21. curiously
22. immediately

Jaime Escalante

1. Did he know?
2. Did he come?
3. Did he work?
4. Did he go?
5. Did he begin?
6. Was it?
7. Did they finish?
8. Did he want?
9. Could they learn?
10. Would he help?
11. Did he open?
12. Did he say?
13. Did he tell?
14. Did they protest?
15. Did he prove?
16. Did they cheat?
17. Did they take?
18. Did they admire?
19. Did it show?
20. Did he change?
21. Did they have?
22. Did they invite?
23. Were they?

Maya Ying Lin and the Vietnam War Memorial

1. They were sent
2. It was published
3. It was divided
4. It was invaded
5. It was lost
6. It was raised
7. It was held
8. It was shown
9. It was approved
10. It was opened
11. They were read

The Ordinary Citizen

1. championship
2. leadership
3. cultural
4. historical
5. scholarship
6. organizational
7. traditional
8. environmental
9. presidential
10. personal
11. friendship
12. national
13. ceremonial
14. membership
15. professional
16. sportsmanship
17. memorial
18. medical, medicinal

Scores

Story	True/False	Self-Test
Betsy Ross	_____	_____ /24
Sacagawea	_____	_____ /25
Dolley Madison	_____	_____ /29
Harriet Beecher Stowe	_____	_____ /35
Abraham Lincoln	_____	_____ /43
Thomas Alva Edison	_____	_____ /47
John Muir	_____	_____ /42
Eleanor Roosevelt	_____	_____ /36
Jackie Robinson	_____	_____ /38
Jonas Salk	_____	_____ /39
Robert Frost	_____	_____ /48
Cesar Chavez	_____	_____ /51
Astronauts	_____	_____ /45
Jaime Escalante	_____	_____ /49
Maya Lin	_____	_____ /38

20th Century Time Line

1901-1909	Theodore Roosevelt presidency - National Parks and wilderness conservation greatly increased
1909	John Muir dies at 76, 12/24. He was born 4/21/1838; visited Yosemite 1868; inspired the founding of the first National Park at Yellowstone 1872.
1917-1918	U.S. fights in World War I.
1929-1941	The Great Depression begins with the collapse of the stock market and ends with WWII.
1931	Thomas Edison dies at 84, 10/18. He was born 2/11/1847; built laboratory at Menlo Park 1876.
1933-1945	Franklin Delano Roosevelt presidency - Eleanor Roosevelt activist First Lady.
1941-1945	U.S. fights in World War II.
1947	Jackie Robinson is the first Black player in Major League Baseball.
1948	United Nations founded. Universal Declaration of Human Rights accepted.
1949	Jackie Robinson named Most Valuable Player in Baseball
1950-1953	U.S. fights in Korean War. 4/27 Armistice leaves Korea divided.
1955	Dr. Jonas Salk's Polio vaccine proves successful. Civil Rights movement gains strength, and Martin Luther King, Jr., is recognized as a leader.
1956	Supreme Court requires U.S. schools to desegregate.
1958	Russia launches *Sputnik*, starting the "Space Race" with the U.S.
1961-1963	John F. Kennedy presidency - Robert Frost reads at his inauguration. Eleanor Roosevelt is chair of Kennedy's Commission on the Status of Women. In 1961, JFK promises that the U.S. will put men on the moon within 10 years.
1962	Eleanor Roosevelt dies at 78. She was born in1884; married FDR in 1905. Jackie Robinson voted into the Baseball Hall of Fame.
1963	Robert Frost dies at 89. He was born 3/26/1874. John Kennedy assassinated at 46, 11/22. He was born 5/29/1917.
1964	President Johnson pushes The Great Society, and Congress passes major civil rights and welfare legislation.
1964-1973	U.S. fights in the Vietnam War, which ended in 1975 with a communist victory.
1965-1970	Cesar Chavez leads a strike of grape pickers and a national boycott on buying grapes.
1968	Martin Luther King and JFK's brother, Robert Kennedy, are assassinated.
1969	U.S. Astronauts land safely on the moon 7/20.
1972	Jackie Robinson dies at 53, 10/24. He was born 1/31/1919.
1974	President Richard Nixon resigns in disgrace after lying to Congress and the American people.
1982	Vietnam War Memorial by 21-year-old Chinese-American Maya Lin is opened on Veterans Day.
1986	AIDS recognized as a world-wide epidemic. Space Shuttle *Challenger* explodes.
1987	Hispanic-American teacher Jaime Escalante becomes famous when a movie shows his life.
1989	The Cold War, which was declared in 1948, ends with U.S.-U.S.S.R. agreements.
1990	U.S. fights *Desert Storm* war against Iraq.
1993	Cesar Chavez dies at 66, 4/22. He was born 3/31/1927.
1995	Dr. Jonas Salk dies at 80, 6/23. He was born 10/28/1914.

Other Materials from Pro Lingua

- **Celebrating American Heroes: Plays for Students of English:** The Playbook
  Celebrating American Heroes: Teacher's Guide (photocopyable)
  Celebrating American Heroes: Cassette
  by Anne Siebert. 13 brief plays about significant historical figures from Sacagawea to Cesar Chavez, from Lincoln, to Edison, to Jackie Robinson. They are designed for reading aloud dramatically. In each play there are a few main characters and a chorus that comments and advises by chanting about the actions of the heroes. Everybody participates. Appropriate for all ages and proficiency levels.

- **American Holidays:** Exploring Traditions, Customs, and Backgrounds
  An intermediate level reader by Barbara Klebanow and Sara Fischer, Ph.D.
  July 4th, Election Day, Christmas, and New Year's Eve: reading about our American national holidays is not only fun, it is a way of exploring our diverse culture and values. How do we celebrate Memorial Day? What is the history of Thanksgiving? What does "Be my valentine" mean? **Special features:** 4 appendices of typical holiday gifts, traditional holiday songs, readings for the holidays, and a listing of other holidays in the U.S. and the official national holiday of each country in the world. **Cassette** available.

- **Potluck:** Exploring American Foods and Meals
  An intermediate reader by Raymond C. Clark
  Potluck presents the vocabulary and culture of our North American cooking and dining, typical U.S. foods and meals, when they are served, regional and specialty foods, tastes, aromas, actions, and implements. This important material is often overlooked in English language texts. **Special features:** for each meal, an illustration showing the way the meal is traditionally served, a list of typical dishes, and a restaurant menu or recipe; a spice and herb chart; a special food index.

- **Living in the United States:** How to Feel at Home, Make Friends, and Enjoy Everyday Life
  An intermediate level guide by Raymond C. Clark and Ani Hawkinson
  This handy, inexpensive cultural-orientation handbook is written for foreign students, visitors, business travelers, and immigrants to the United States. It includes information on food and restaurants, drinking and smoking laws, hotels, and communications. There are sections on Customs and Values (including tips on business etiquette) and History and Country Facts (including information on Technology and Change). The appendix on the 50 states gives comparative statistical and political information.

- **Conversation Strategies:** Pair and Group Activities for Developing Communicative Competence
  by David Kehe and Peggy Dustin Kehe. This is an integrated skills student text for intermediate level students, although it works well with more advanced students who don't know the strategies. There are 24 activities giving practice with the words, phrases, and conventions used to maintain effective control of conversations. Strategies include polite forms, correction, agreement and disagreement, summarization, interruptions, and avoiding conversation killers.

- **Discussion Strategies:** Beyond Everyday Conversation by the Kehes. This is an integrated skills text providing clear, step-by-step, focused practice of 13 discussion skills needed in academic and business situations.

Pro Lingua Associates

P.O. Box 1348, Brattleboro, VT 05302 • 800-366-4775 • Webstore www.ProLinguaAssociates.com